Biblical Crisis Counseling:
Not If, But When

Dr. John Babler

Copyright © 2014 by John Babler
All rights reserved. No part of this publication may be reproduced in any form without prior permission.

ISBN-13: 978-1503284241
ISBN: 1503284247

Biblical Crisis Counseling:
Not If, But When

Unless otherwise indicated, Bible quotations in this publication are taken from the New American Standard Bible, © 1960, 1962, 1963, 1971, 1972, 1973, 1975, 1977, 1995 by the Lockman Foundation.
Used by permission.

Table of Contents

Crisis: Up Close and Personal 1

Dealing with Crisis: Not If, But When 13

Biblical Theology for Crisis Ministry 19

Crisis in Scripture 26

Job, Joseph, and Jonah: Three Men in Crisis 35

Biblical Crisis Intervention 44

Responding to Crisis 55

Disaster Relief and the Church 77

Foreword

I am thankful for many who have worked "behind the scenes" to bring about the completion of this book. First and foremost, my wife of over thirty years has been a great source of support, wisdom, and encouragement to me. I have frequently been pulled away from her and our children to respond to the crises that have given me a unique perspective in addressing this topic. With courage, love, and tenacity she has borne the brunt of my absences. Her education and experience in ministering in crisis frequently occurred while I was away and the kids had their own crises – broken arms, conflicts with friends, etc.

My friend and colleague, Dr. David Penley worked together with me to develop the Biblical Crisis Intervention Model in the aftermath of the Wedgwood Baptist Church shooting. His research and writing form the basis for some of what you will read. Dr. Mike Bizzell worked on pulling much of this information together into a readable format many years ago while he was a Ph.D. student. Finally, Dale Johnson, Cheryl Bell, and Sam Stephens three of our current Ph.D. students, have written and edited as well as made valuable suggestions for this book.

I know that in the midst of crisis there are many opportunities to minister the love of God and His compassion. It is my prayer that this book will help you catch the vision of this possibility to impact people in the midst of sometimes unimaginable situations and begin the process of equipping you to do so in a way that honors God (1 Cor. 10:31).

Minister the Word!

John Babler

1

Crisis: Up Close And Personal

When I was sixteen years old, my older brother David had a party a few days before his twenty-fifth birthday. He was in a motorcycle gang and the party included members of the gang and his girlfriend. He invited me to stop by early in the evening – before things got too wild. I went for a short time and visited with him and his friends. On the way home I stopped at our neighborhood 7-Eleven and was hanging out with some of my friends when my Dad called looking for me. I was surprised, as my Dad had never tracked me down before. He asked me to come home right away. Mom had just had surgery and was recovering and I thought it had something to do with her. When I got home Dad told me that the police had called and that they thought David had been in a motorcycle wreck and been killed, but they had not yet made a positive identification. While Mom was asleep we spent the next hour, which seemed like an eternity, trying to talk ourselves into believing that this was a mistake and this unidentified man wasn't my brother. Once the police officer came to the door, confirmed our worst fears, and gave us David's personal effects, our family was changed forever. David was buried on his birthday.

Just before Thanksgiving over ten years later, while I was a seminary student, another call came. Mom, who was recovering from a mastectomy due to a recent cancer diagnosis, called and told me that my other brother, Mark, had collapsed and been taken by ambulance to the hospital. Mark had his share of crises. Born legally blind with no iris, he had been adopted by my parents when he was two years old. As an adult he married, had a career in restaurant management and then went on to complete a college degree in rehabilitation science so he could help others. Mark, however, struggled with drinking. His sin led to a divorce and ultimately the loss of almost everything. At that point Dad took him to the Salvation Army's rehab program. Mark completed the program and was then hired to manage the food service for the Salvation Army in Dallas.

Piecing together details after the fact, it appears that during the week of Thanksgiving, Mark was both stressed and physically ill. The General of the U.S. Salvation Army was coming for a visit and Mark was to prepare a brunch in addition to preparing Thanksgiving meals for all the residents, staff, and families. Some of the old-timers had shared that when they couldn't get alcohol they substituted Sterno, which is a fuel used in the food industry for buffet heating. In an effort to get through the week, Mark ingested about a teaspoon, but what he did not know was that when the body processes Sterno it produces the same toxin that is in bee stings. Mark was highly allergic to bee stings and his allergic reaction caused his brain to swell and, within days, to quit functioning. Mark died on the day before Thanksgiving. After committing his life to Christ while in the program, he had been scheduled to be formally inducted into the church on the following Sunday.

My mother's fight with cancer continued another two years. She finally came to an end of her treatment options and was at peace with the fact that she was dying. She lived long enough to see me graduate from seminary and begin a position at a children's home in Amarillo and to meet her second grandchild. A few months after we had moved to Amarillo, we came back to be with her during her final days. It was a hard, yet very vital time. In typical fashion, she waited for us to leave to go back to Amarillo and passed on hours after we left. I don't think she wanted to die with us there.

As a parent, crisis can be up-close and personal, too. One of our children spent three days in the Neonatal Intensive Care Unit (NICU). As with most crises, everything had to be flexible. We rearranged our schedules so that one of us could be with him at the hospital around the clock, our other children were concerned and needed support, and the impact on ministry, the other children, and us was significant. The recognition of children as a gift from God and the reminder of life's fragility were particularly poignant during this time.

Even as my children have grown up into adulthood and grandchildren have entered the picture, crises have continued to provide challenges and blessings. One of the biggest challenges for me was when life and death crises have occurred and there was nothing I could do to protect my children or grandchildren. My oldest son, Hudson, and I were volunteer firefighters together for a number of years (he is now a full time firefighter with Dallas Fire-Rescue). When I retired as Fire Chief he resigned from the department as well due to various time constraints. One morning at about 3:30 I received a call from Hudson, who with his wife and daughter lived two miles from us in seminary housing. He said there had been a small fire in their home and was wondering if I could come over. Pulling up to their house, I saw firefighters throwing charred, burnt furniture out of the upstairs window of my granddaughter's room. I realized that this was no small fire.

Hudson's wife, Molly, tells the story in her own words:

> *At three a.m. I awoke with a start when I heard the lightning strike a tree. Never have I heard a strike that close before! It sounded like it was the tree*

outside my window, so I got up to check it (I was afraid of it breaking our window if the tree split). I didn't see anything . . . my Husband was awake and headed to the bathroom as I gazed at the sky from the window. All of the sudden he bounded back and sharply yelled "get your clothes on!" I obeyed (I had NEVER heard him use such a tone before) and he explained as he dressed that he could smell smoke and was thinking that perhaps a fire had started in our townhome's attic space after the strike. I pulled on something in the dark (later I found out it was inside out and backwards) and I reached my infant daughter's room just as Hudson was opening the door. The sight I saw when the door was thrown open was something I never hope to see again. Fire lashed out at us, and engulfed the entire room. It flashed over the ceiling and licked at us overhead. We stepped back and fell to our knees from the sight. I remember a sound coming out of my husband that was something of a moan and a shriek - it was terrible and I just knew that our sweet baby was gone. We couldn't see her. We couldn't see the crib. All we saw were the flames encircling the room from floor to ceiling. I stood frozen. The heat was tremendous. All of the sudden my husband was gone. Into the flames. Everything was slow motion. I couldn't see my husband or my baby. And then, just as quick as he had gone, there he was -- holding our child in his arms and then he urged me down the stairs and out the door. As we left the house, we finally heard the smoke detector sound an alert.

As we rushed outside, I looked at our baby, afraid of what I might see. I grabbed her into my arms while my husband called 911 and started banging on all our neighbors doors to alert them. What I will never forget is the smell that permeated my daughter that morning - baby soap. My husband and I smelled like soot and cinder - I think it took my hair over a week to lose the smoke smell and my husband's beautiful, long, eyelashes had been scorched off. But as I held my sweet twelve month old child, the only smell coming from her sweet little head and body was of the baby soap from her bath the night before. She didn't even have soot on her little nightgown. We had her checked out by the paramedics, and she was perfect.

My daughter had been in the flames that night - and when my husband reached in and groped for her and passed her back through, she was not scorched. When we went back in later, after the firemen had put out the flames, we saw her crib. Her bedding was melted to the frame and it was a sooty, scorched mess. But there, in the center of the crib, was a small form, perfectly clean and white where my daughter had lain. I know that the Lord showed us His hand of protection that night - not just for my daughter, but all three of us. We had passed through the flames and we were safe. We lost everything upstairs, and most of our furniture downstairs because of the smoke damage, yet the Lord spared us and we were beyond joyful.

This is just one example of how the Lord has passed our family through the flames and brought us safely to the other side. Many of these times have been intangible, yet flames of life that we were struggling through - that we just didn't think we would make it out of. Yet the Lord has always brought this instance back to my heart and I know that day he told me, "You see, I am here. I am with you. And there will never be a storm that you will go through, that I will not see you safely through." This has been a balm of peace over my heart since that day. You see, I know that whether I live or die, my Lord will be with me, and will walk with me until I am safely home.

About two years after this incident, Hudson called me while I was in Houston teaching for a week. I was leaving the hotel for class and he asked if he could stop by my house on the way to his and borrow a gun. Molly had called him and said someone was breaking into the house. My fear for what might happen was only matched in intensity by my frustration at being five hours away and not being able to do anything to help. The man did end up breaking in the house and Molly locked herself and both of their daughters in a closet. (The story of how there was a closet door with a lock on it in the house is a testimony to God's provision for the protection of Molly and the girls!)

Molly tells the story of this crisis in her personal blog:

HOME INVASION - January 4, 2011
I thought I heard a male voice, but it was so soft and voices really carry in our neighborhood. I checked the house thinking maybe Ava had upset something when she woke up and maybe something dropped out of her bed. Didn't see anything . . . didn't hear anything else. I call Hudson and tell him about the noise and he tells me to pull the gun out of the safe we have and that he would come and check things out. I am feeling calmer at this point because I haven't heard a noise for about ten minutes. . .

Suddenly I see a shadow in our back yard through the girls' bedroom curtain . . . the girls share a room and the crib sits against a window. I then hear several thuds against the window . . . and I KNOW someone is out there trying to get in! Ava starts screaming. . . I reached for the cell phone while carrying the gun (safety still on) and Claire and instinctively called Hudson. ... as Hudson answered the glass started breaking and I frantically told Hudson someone was breaking in. He screamed CALL 911!! The dispatcher tells me to find somewhere I can lock myself and the girls up and hide. I then realize that the ONLY place we have to hide is Hudson's and my closet since it has a turn lock on the inside part and a key lock on the outside. We had been meaning to fix this because it was a mistake as it was supposed to be installed on the bathroom door... so I quickly sequester us in the closet, lock the door, put Ava in the back corner behind me and open the dresser drawer to place Claire in so she would be safe behind me. I took the safety off the gun and stood in position as I hear the glass finally break all the way through... a sharp THUD and then the closet door handle starts JIGGLING!!!! He came right to us and attempted to come through the door! By then, the dispatcher told me the police were coming on scene as I told her I had a gun and he was trying to get into the closet...

THEN, I hear him take off running out of the house... Hudson thinks he waited to see if I would come out of the closet... then he heard the sirens... Hudson said he had just pulled up before the police arrived on scene and saw the man run out of our house, THROUGH THE FRONT DOOR... WITH A CROW BAR... HOP OVER OUR NEIGHBORS FENCE... and DISAPPEAR. No finger prints... He by-passed our TV, our Wii, a Mac laptop, a gun safe and came directly to us... he heard the girls crying through the broken glass, and he still came. He came right to the closet and tried to get in. The Lord placed his hand on us once again and I believe he spared us from something very evil this morning... This man was not after money or electronics. The police told us that in every instance where criminals break in to steal, they do so thinking no one is home... in the instance someone is home, they don't care if you are hiding, they take what they can carry and run. Praise the

Lord for watching over us and giving us safety!

These and other personal crises that we have dealt with have provided clear application of Romans 8:28-29:

> *And we know that God causes all things to work together for good to those who love God, to those who are called according to His purpose. For those whom He foreknew, He also predestined to become conformed to the image of His Son, so that He would be the firstborn among many brethren . . .*[1]

Many times Christians encounter Romans 8:28 in isolation. The problem with this is that we always try to insert some sense of our personal definition of *good* into the verse. Verse 29 is essential because it provides the definition of the good God brings as He causes all things to work together. It is that we might become conformed to the image of His Son! God has assuredly worked all the above out for good as He has used it to make me and many others more like Christ, more conformed to His image.

I have had the honor of being in vocational Christian ministry for over thirty years. During that time most of my positions have provided regular opportunities to help and counsel hurting people in a variety of crises. I have ministered in inner-city missions, a residential children's home, in hospice, and as a hospital chaplain. While serving as a professor at Southwestern Baptist Theological Seminary, I have had opportunities to counsel frequently with students and colleagues as they have encountered crises. During my time at Southwestern I have also served as a volunteer fire fighter, chaplain, fire chief, and even now continue to serve with the Texas Corps of Fire Chaplains and the Texas Line of Duty Task Force.

---

[1] Unless otherwise noted, all Scripture quotations are from the New American Standard Bible.

In the midst of these ministry roles, I have had opportunities to deal with people in both common and very uncommon crises. In 1999, a gunman entered Wedgwood Baptist Church in Fort Worth and either killed or wounded fourteen individuals before taking his own life. I was able to respond as a fire chaplain and minister to some of the first responders as well as assisting with death notifications that lasted into the early morning. The day after the shooting I was invited to a neighboring high school that had been impacted by the shooting. A group of seventeen students from this school had attended the rally the night before and one of them was killed and another wounded. I gathered a small group of seminary students and we went to the school. We were able to not only comfort those high school students in the name of Christ, but to openly share the Gospel in a public school!

After the Virginia Tech shooting I was able to respond and work out of a local church to provide biblical counsel to those who had been impacted by that crisis. I was able to spend a week in New Orleans immediately following Hurricane Katrina serving as a fire chaplain and then I led our church to form a partnership with a church that had been devastated by Katrina. This partnership lasted more than one year and provided opportunities for our members to serve and gave me a greater understanding of the dynamics of long-term rebuilding. In my ministry with the Texas Line of Duty Death Task Force, I have responded and ministered in the midst of many line-of-duty deaths of emergency service personnel, most recently in the context of the fertilizer plant explosion in West, Texas where twelve firefighters died.

My personal and ministerial experiences with crisis form the foundation upon which the words in the following chapters have been crafted. It is my prayer that God uses this book to help you minister effectively during times of crisis. Minister the Word!

WHAT IS BIBLICAL COUNSELING?

In simple terms, *Biblical Counseling* is ministering Scripture to those who face struggles in life or who desire wisdom or God's direction. Biblical Counseling is not a new concept. There are examples throughout the pages of Scripture where God's Word is cited in instructive and corrective ways to both individuals and groups. There are also examples throughout church history of the utilization of Scripture by pastors and others to provide encouragement and admonition to members of the flock.

In the midst of a therapeutic-centric culture, counseling has become a formal, professional discipline.[2] Jay Adams is credited with "re-discovering" Biblical Counseling. In his book *Competent to Counsel,* first published in 1970, Adams utilized the term *nouthetic*, which is transliterated from the Greek New Testament word that is most frequently translated as admonish, to describe counseling that focuses on sharing Scripture by speaking the truth in love to those in need of counsel.

Since *Competent to Counsel* was published, many books, pamphlets, training centers, undergraduate and graduate degree programs for Biblical Counseling have been developed. During the first thirty years since the publication of this landmark work there was relatively clear demarcation and respectful debate between Biblical Counseling and what is often described as Christian Counseling. During the last ten years lines have become blurred as some of those in the Biblical Counseling arena have focused significant energies on developing relationships with other counselors. In turn these Christian Counselors have begun to identify themselves

---

[2] In some ways the term counseling could include several disciplines including: psychiatry, psychology, social work, and marriage/family therapy.

as Biblical Counselors. This has resulted in growing confusion as to the definition and nature of Biblical Counseling.

I have had the opportunity to read and reflect on many recent attempts to define Biblical Counseling by those who consider themselves to be Biblical Counselors. To my surprise, many of these definitions missed key foundational elements. None of them mention sin or repentance, only one refers to a conviction regarding the sufficiency of Scripture, and they are all broad enough to allow many who hold contradicting philosophies to adopt the title of Biblical Counselor.

Based on these reflections and many years of personal experience teaching students how to minister Scripture, I believe the following definition holds true to the essential nature, practice, and purpose of Biblical Counseling:

Biblical Counseling is a ministry of the local church whereby transformed believers in Christ (John 3:3-8) who are indwelled, empowered, and led by the Holy Spirit (John 14:26) minister the living and active Word of God (Heb. 4:12) to others in view of evangelizing the lost and teaching the saved (Matt. 28:18-20). Biblical Counseling is based on the conviction that Scripture is sufficient for the counseling task and superior to anything the world has to offer (2 Tim. 3:16-17; Heb. 4:12; 2 Peter 1:3-4; Ps. 119; James 4:4). Biblical counselors realize the significance of sin (Rom. 3:23, 6:23) and after self-confrontation (Matt. 7:5) lovingly confront those who are in sin (Luke 17:3-4) and call them to repentance (2 Tim. 2:24-26). Biblical counselors also realize that in a fallen world people can face significant crises that are not a direct result of their own personal sin (Job 1-2). Biblical counselors purposefully and patiently walk with, serve, love, encourage, and help people in these cases (1 Th. 5:14). They also call upon others in the church to assist based on their gifts and roles (1 Cor. 12:4-31).

Biblical counseling can be informal, accomplished over coffee, in the hallways of the church, or in the work place and community. It can also be formal, accomplished through scheduled appointments in an office setting. All Christians should be taught to minister God's Word and boldly do so in the context of the local church. Biblical counselors are motivated by the compassion of Christ (Mt. 9:36, 2 Cor. 5:14-15) and through obeying His commands, (John 14:21) seek to be salt and light in such a way that others see their good works and glorify their Father in heaven (Mt. 5:16).

This definition forms the foundation for the approach to crisis counseling contained in the pages that follow.

Dealing with Crisis: Not if – But when

THE NATURE OF CRISIS

What comes to your mind when you think about the word *crisis*? Words such as, "chaos," "pain," "fear," "anxiety," "loss," "hopeless," "trauma," and "death" would be representative of our initial responses. Most people have experienced some type of personal crisis and certainly are at least aware through the media of the devastation of large-scale disasters.

It is the focus of this book to challenge Christians to consider that crises provide opportunities. The first, and most obvious, is to glorify and honor God. We can learn how to trust in the Lord's provision fully and to grow in our relationship with Him. We are also given the opportunity to love and serve others in the name of Christ and to minister His Word.

Man-Made Crisis

The world is becoming increasingly violent. It seems that no one is safe and no place is beyond the reach of the violence that permeates society. The boundaries of safety have been breached in places ranging from movie theaters, to schools, and even churches. Shooters enter churches gunning down innocent people. Incidents involving gun-violence such as that at Columbine High School or Sandy Hook Elementary are seemingly commonplace today. We hear of road and airline rage episodes daily and we have even watched in horror as buildings are brought to the ground by terrorists while television brings the grotesque reality of ethnic wars and natural disasters into our homes on a regular basis. The advanced technology of our present age has allowed us to become virtual victims of crime, war, and natural disaster. Images of the war on terror in Iraq and Afghanistan and suffering associated with the Indonesian tsunami and other disasters are etched in the minds of many of us.

Natural Disasters

Natural disasters seem to bring more questions to our mind than answers. In the aftermath of Hurricane Katrina, we became painfully aware of the emotional, physical, and economic effects of disaster. Small towns like Joplin, Missouri and Moore, Oklahoma could attest to the devastation of tornados. Like Katrina, these disasters have opened our eyes to the fact that local churches and individual Christians must be prepared to respond to disaster in a skillful and timely manner.

Personal Crisis

Personal crises abound. Divorce divides families and often leaves emotional debris in its wake. Drugs and alcohol take their toll on children and parents alike. Teens and children are becoming increasingly involved in crime and violence. According to the National Vital Statistics Report published by the Center for Disease Control, in 2008 there were 36,909 suicides in America. The FBI reports that there were over one million violent crimes reported. Over 750,000 teens become pregnant each year and nearly 27% of teen pregnancies end in abortion.[3]

The direct effect of crisis can seem removed from us, especially in light of the sometimes numbing effect that comes with frequent media reports of violence and disaster. In the face of such overwhelming numbers, we must remember that these statistics represent human beings thrust

---

[3]For more information regarding these statistics see, The Alan Guttmacher Institute: http://www.agiusa.org/pubs/teen_stats.html

into uncertainty, turmoil, anxiety, and fear. These are men and women that we are called by God to love and serve. Scripture instructs us to do everything as unto the Lord (Col. 3:23.) In the following pages, we will review the mandates of the Bible in order to develop a biblical model for crisis intervention and ministry.

CRISIS DEFINED

In their book *Critical Incident Stress Management,* Everly and Mitchell technically define crisis as "an acute disruption of psychological homeostasis wherein one's usual coping mechanisms fail and there exists evidence of distress and functional impairment."

The word *crisis* comes from Greek the *krisis,* which literally means decision. According to Merriam-Webster a crisis can be, **a:** "the turning point for better or worse in an acute disease or fever," **b:** "a paroxysmal attack of pain, distress, or disordered function," **c:** "an emotionally significant event or radical change of status in a person's life," **d:** "the decisive moment (as in a literary plot)," **e:** "an unstable or crucial time or state of affairs in which a decisive change is impending; *especially*: one with the distinct possibility of a highly undesirable outcome," **f:** "a situation that has reached a critical phase."

The most common characterization of a crisis involves an unstable situation of extreme danger or difficulty or a crucial stage or turning point in the course of an event.

AN OPPORTUNITY TO GLORIFY GOD

God's self-disclosure has revealed His compassion for the hurting. The Old Testament law made provision for the poor and helpless in the land (Ex. 22:25-27; Lev. 19:9-10; Deut. 14:28-29). The prophets warned Israel that they were not to take advantage of the helpless (Zech. 7:10). Jesus commanded his followers to show compassion for others in the parable of the Good Samaritan (Luke 10:29-37). In Matthew 25, Jesus emphasized the importance of ministering to the hurting and needy. Jesus' life provides the example and mandate for every believer to be involved in ministry. Ministry is vitally connected to Christ's command to love God supremely and love others as we love ourselves (Matt. 22:34-40). This answers *why* we do ministry. Still, we must answer the question of the ultimate purpose of ministry. Jesus answered this question during the Sermon on the Mount, when He said, "let your light so shine before men that they may see your good works and *glorify your Father in Heaven* [emphasis added]" (Matt. 5:16).

Throughout the Gospel of John, Jesus spoke of his mission to glorify the Father (John 11:4; 12:28; 14:13; 17:1). Paul reminded believers in 1 Corinthians 10:31 to "do all you do to the glory of God." Peter said that those who minister should do it in the ability God gives them that "in all things God may be glorified through Jesus Christ . . ." (1 Peter 4:11). Ultimately, all Christian ministries must glorify God through Jesus Christ. When this happens people are brought to faith in Christ and their relationship with him is strengthened. Because crises bring about the need to make many decisions, Christians are afforded opportunities to glorify God by making choices and acting in ways that honor Him.

We bring glory to God by making decisions that portray our belief in and dependence on the sovereignty of God in all circumstances.

Some boast in chariots and some in horses, But we will boast in the name of the Lord, our God. Psalm 20:7

For our heart rejoices in Him, Because we trust in His holy name. Psalm 33:21

Trust in the LORD with all your heart and do not lean on your own understanding. Proverbs 3:5

Trust in the LORD forever, For in God the Lord, we have an everlasting Rock. Isaiah 26:4

*Though the flock should be cut off from the fold
And there be no cattle in the stalls,
Yet I will exult in the LORD,
I will rejoice in the God of my salvation.
The LORD GOD is my strength,
And He has made my feet like hinds' feet,
And makes me walk on my high places.
Habakkuk 3:17-19*

We bring glory to God by taking action that replicates in the lives of others the same love and compassionate comfort God offers us as his children.

Blessed be the God and Father of our Lord Jesus Christ, the Father of mercies and God of all comfort, who comforts us in all our affliction so that we will be able to comfort those who are in any affliction with the comfort with which we ourselves are comforted by God. 2 Corinthians 1:3-4

Rejoice with those who rejoice, and weep with those who weep. Romans 12:15

Bear one another's burdens, and thereby fulfill the law of Christ. Galatians 6:2

*We urge you, brethren, admonish the unruly, encourage the fainthearted, help the weak, be patient with everyone.
1 Thessalonians 5:14*

We bring glory to God when we endure suffering and hardship faithfully.

. . . therefore, we ourselves speak proudly of you among the churches of God for your perseverance and faith in the midst of all your persecutions and afflictions which you endure. 2 Thessalonians 1:4.

Therefore, those also who suffer according to the will of God shall entrust their souls to a faithful Creator in doing what is right. 1 Peter 4:19

And He has said to me, "My grace is sufficient for you, for power is perfected in weakness." Most gladly, therefore, I will rather boast about my weaknesses, so that the power of Christ may dwell in me. 2 Corinthians 12:9

Biblical Theology for Crisis Ministry

And we know that God causes all things to work together for good to those who love God, to those who are called according to His purpose. For those whom He foreknew, He also predestined to become conformed to the image of His Son, so that He would be the firstborn among many brethren. Romans 8:28-29.

Why are we plagued by disaster and crisis? God's Word reveals three causes of crisis and disaster: Sin, Satan's temptations, and God's testing.

SIN

We live in a sinful and fallen world. Crisis in an individual's life may be the result of his personal sin, the sin of others, the sin of society, or the effects of original sin and the Fall (which permeate, corrupt, and frustrate our world.)

Original Sin

When Adam disobeyed God, all of creation was corrupted by sin. Death entered the world and man's environment became hostile toward him. Ultimately, all suffering can be traced back to the effects of original sin.

Then to Adam He said, "Because you have listened to the voice of your wife, and have eaten from the tree about which I commanded you, saying, 'You shall not eat from it'; Cursed is the ground because of you; In toil you will eat of it All the days of your life. "Both thorns and thistles it shall grow for you; And you will eat the plants of the field; By the sweat of your face you will eat bread, till you return to the ground, because from it you were taken; For you are dust, And to dust you shall return." Genesis 3:17-19

Therefore, just as through one man sin entered into the world, and death through sin, and so death spread to all men, because all sinned . . . Romans 5:12

For the creation was subjected to futility, not willingly, but because of Him who subjected it, in hope that the creation itself also will be set free from its slavery to corruption into the freedom of the glory of the children of God. For we know that the whole creation groans and suffers the pains of childbirth together until now. Romans 8:20-22

Now on the same occasion there were some present who reported to Him about the Galileans whose blood Pilate had mixed with their sacrifices. And Jesus said to them, "Do you suppose that these Galileans were greater sinners than all other Galileans because they suffered this fate? I tell you, no, but unless you repent, you will all likewise perish. Or do you suppose that those eighteen on whom the tower in Siloam fell and killed them were worse culprits than all the men who live in Jerusalem? I tell you, no, but unless you repent, you will all likewise perish." Luke 13:1-5

Personal Sin

Many times personal sin precipitates crisis in the lives of individuals. When one ignores God's commands, he inevitably faces the consequences of his sin. Consider the prodigal son as a prime example (Luke 15:11-19). At other times, people suffer due to the sinful acts of others.

Do not be deceived, God is not mocked; for whatever a man sows, this he will also reap. For the one who sows to his own flesh will from the flesh reap corruption, but the one who

*sows to the Spirit will from the Spirit reap eternal life.
Galatians 6:7-8*

*For all have sinned and fall short of the glory of God.
Romans 3:23*

Let no one say when he is tempted, "I am being tempted by God"; for God cannot be tempted by evil, and He Himself does not tempt anyone. But each one is tempted when he is carried away and enticed by his own lust. Then when lust has conceived, it gives birth to sin; and when sin is accomplished, it brings forth death. James 1:13-15

The heart is more deceitful than all else, and is desperately sick; who can understand it? Jeremiah 17:9

*Alexander the coppersmith did me much harm; the Lord will repay him according to his deeds. Be on guard against him yourself, for he vigorously opposed our teaching.
2 Timothy 4:14-15*

Indeed, all who desire to live godly in Christ Jesus will be persecuted. 2 Timothy 3:12

SATAN'S TEMPTATIONS

Satan is at work and attempts to destroy God's representations in the world. Scripture teaches that Satan has the ability disrupt our lives with pain and suffering as he works through his associates and the worldly power structure.

Finally, be strong in the Lord and in the strength of His might. Put on the full armor of God, so that you will be able to stand firm against the schemes of the devil. For our struggle is not against flesh and blood, but against the rulers, against the powers, against the world forces of this darkness, against the spiritual forces of wickedness in the heavenly places. Ephesians 6:10-12

Be of sober spirit, be on the alert Your adversary, the devil, prowls around like a roaring lion, seeking someone to devour. 1 Peter 5:8

Simon, Simon, behold, Satan has demanded permission to sift you like wheat. Luke 22:31

You are of your father the devil, and you want to do the desires of your father. He was a murderer from the beginning, and does not stand in the truth because there is no truth in him. Whenever he speaks a lie, he speaks from his own nature, for he is a liar and the father of lies. John 8:44

The thief comes only to steal and kill and destroy; I came that they may have life, and have it abundantly. John 10:10

I have decided to deliver such a one to Satan for the destruction of his flesh, so that his spirit may be saved in the day of the Lord Jesus. 1 Corinthians 5:5

No temptation has overtaken you but such as is common to man; and God is faithful, who will not allow you to be tempted beyond what you are able, but with the temptation will provide a way of escape also, so that you will be able to endure it. 1 Corinthians 10:13

Because of the surpassing greatness of the revelations, for this reason, to keep me from exalting myself, there was given me a thorn in the flesh, a messenger of Satan to torment me- to keep me from exalting myself! 2 Corinthians 12:7

GOD'S TESTING

God does not tempt, but He may test His people. Although Scripture speaks of this testing, God does not tempt believers to fall into sin. God's testing is ultimately designed for our sanctification and His glory. In His omniscience, God certainly does not need to see how faithful we are. In the end, God's testing reveals to us how weak we are and how faithful He is. When we respond faithfully to the suffering and hardships of life, God is glorified, we are sanctified, and others are drawn to Christ.

Isaac spoke to Abraham his father and said, "My father!" And he said, "Here I am, my son." And he said, "Behold, the fire and the wood, but where is the lamb for the burnt offering?" Abraham said, "God will provide for Himself the lamb for the burnt offering, my son." So the two of them walked on together. Then they came to the place of which God had told him; and Abraham built the altar there and arranged the wood, and bound his son Issac and laid him on the altar, on top of the wood. Abraham stretched out his hand and took the knife to slay his son. But the angel of the Lord called to him from heaven and said, "Abraham, Abraham!" And he said, "Do not stretch out your hand against the lad, and do nothing to him; for now I know that you fear God, since you have not withheld your son, your only son, from Me." Then Abraham raised his eyes and looked, and behold, behind him a ram caught in the thicket by his horns; and Abraham went and took the ram and offered him up for a burnt offering in the place of his son. Abraham called the name of that place The Lord Will Provide, as it is said to this day, "In the mount of the Lord it will be provided." Genesis 22:7-14

Then the LORD said to Moses, "Behold, I will rain bread from heaven for you; and the people shall go out and gather a day's portion every day, that I may test them, whether or not they will walk in My instruction." Exodus 16:4

I also will no longer drive out before them any of the nations which Joshua left when he died, in order to test Israel by them, whether they will keep the way of the LORD to walk in it as their fathers did, or not. Judges 2:21-22

And I will bring the third part through the fire, Refine them as silver is refined ,And test them as gold is tested They will call on My name, And I will answer them; I will say, "They are My people," And they will say, "The LORD is my God." Zechariah 13:9

Consider it all joy, my brethren, when you encounter various trials, knowing that the testing of your faith produces endurance. And let endurance have its perfect result, so that you may be perfect and complete, lacking in nothing. But if any of you lacks wisdom, let him ask of God, who gives to all generously and without reproach, and it will be given to him. James 1:2-5

But if you are without discipline, of which all have become partakers, then you are illegitimate children and not sons. Furthermore, we had earthly fathers to discipline us, and we respected them; shall we not much rather be subject to the Father of spirits and live? For they disciplined us for a short time as seemed best to them, but he disciplines us for our good, so that we may share in His holiness. All discipline for the moment seems not to be joyful, but sorrowful; yet to those who have been trained by it, afterwards it yields the peaceful fruit of righteousness. Hebrews 12:8-11

For this finds favor, if for the sake of conscience toward God a person bears up under sorrows when suffering unjustly. For what credit is there if, when you sin and are harshly treated, you endure it with patience? But if when you do what is right and suffer for it you patiently endure it, this finds favor with God. 1 Peter 2:19-20

Do not worry then, saying, "What will we eat?" or "What will we drink?" or "What will we wear for clothing?" For the Gentiles eagerly seek all these things; for your heavenly Father knows that you need all these things. "But seek first His kingdom and His righteousness, and all these things will be added to you. Matthew 6:31-33

Trials and temptations, circumstances and the sins of others are not the ultimate issue. When trials, temptation, disaster, personal sin, or anything else bring us to a point of crisis, how we respond – the decisions we make and action we take – will either reflect a faithful, obedient, God honoring heart or a doubtful, self-centered one.

Crisis in Scripture

Hear me when I call, O God of my righteousness! You have relieved me in my distress; have mercy on me and hear my prayer. Psalm 4:1

As we have seen, even a casual reading of the Bible reveals that man has faced crises since Adam's fall and will continue to face them with ever-increasing frequency and intensity until Christ's return. God, through His Word, makes it clear that He cares about people in crisis. The Bible contains varied responses to crisis by all kinds of people from all walks of life. It relates the struggles of both believers and unbelievers as they wrestle with crisis and the stresses that accompany it. Many passages reveal God's commands and principles necessary for dealing with crisis effectively. A study of crisis in the Bible shows that a biblical view of crisis is not a blanket approach. Consider the following examples of crisis found in the Bible.

THE PARABLE OF THE GOOD SAMARITAN: LUKE 10: 30-37

In this parable, a man is attacked, robbed, and left for dead. The crime brings both bodily injury and economic loss (v. 30). The man is left helpless, naked, and dying by the side of the road to Jericho. The crisis is unexpected and the man is in need of emergency assistance. What happened is not the fault of the victim and can only be attributed to the sin in the lives of the criminals. Many situations we encounter today involve similar circumstances. Sometimes people are victims of violent crimes and require medical attention, but more often we will deal with the emotional and spiritual effects of crime in the lives of people. Occasionally, crime will produce economic needs in the lives of victims, and we may be able to bring relief.

The reaction to this particular crisis is varied. A priest crosses the road to avoid even looking at the man (vs. 31). He does not even stop to appraise the situation. He chooses to remain ignorant and uninvolved. The Levite does stop and observe, but he too decides to pass by on the other side (vs. 32). Many times, people today, even Christians, react with similar ignorance and disinterest when it comes to ministering to people in crisis. We can best glorify God when we are willing to get involved in the lives of hurting people.

Finally, a Samaritan man sees the wounded victim, has compassion on him, applies first-aid, transports the man to a place of recovery, pays for the man's expenses, and promises to follow up (vs. 33-35). The Samaritan's reaction of compassion is commended by Jesus. Christians today could learn much from the Samaritan. He crossed racial and social barriers, accepted inconvenience, and committed time, resources, and money in ministering to the injured man. Finally, and of great importance, he promised to follow up and return to invest more in the ministry if necessary.

There is no stated purpose for the crisis in this story. The cause of the crisis is the sin of others. Providing a broad definition of "neighbor" and an example of how God's people should show God's love seems to be the goal of this parable. Christ makes it clear that the Samaritan's actions are to serve as an example for God's people (vs. 37). Throughout the New Testament, the words Jesus spoke to the expert of the law when he identified a hated Samaritan as his neighbor, are reiterated over and over; "Go and do likewise."

THE DEATH OF LAZARUS: JOHN 11:1-45

The crisis in this account is that of sickness and death. Lazarus fell sick and his sisters, Mary and Martha, sent for Jesus (vs. 1-3). He waited two days before he began the journey to Bethany (vs. 5-7). By that time, Lazarus had died (vs. 14). When Jesus arrived, Lazarus had already been in the tomb four days (vs.17). Mary and Martha were heartbroken at the death of their brother and because it had taken Jesus so long to respond (vs. 19-21).

Jesus responded to this crisis with recognition and calm trust in the ultimate plan of God. When Jesus arrived and witnessed the sorrow of his friends he responded with tears of compassion. Mary and Martha had initially turned to the person they believed could help in the situation. When Lazarus died they responded with sorrow and mourning. Mary and Martha, along with the friends who were mourning with them, asked if Jesus could not have saved the life of Lazarus (vs. 37).

We can learn from Jesus' example to trust the ultimate purposes of God when ministering to others in the crisis of sickness and death. Though we will never possess the perfect knowledge that Jesus had, we can learn to follow the lead of the Holy Spirit and sense when to take immediate action and when to wait on the Lord. People will always ask why their loved ones have died. We must learn how to field such questions with sensitivity, while pointing those in grief toward the sovereignty and grace of God.

The ministry that occurred in this story is two-fold. Jesus came to Mary and Martha through words of encouragement and visual compassion. He called upon them to trust God (vs. 40). Jesus saw the big picture from the beginning (vs. 4). He ultimately raised Lazarus and brought him forth from the tomb (vs. 43-44). We certainly cannot go around raising people from the dead, but we can learn something about ministering to people in crisis from this passage. It is important to remain calm in crisis and trust the sovereignty of God. A clear display of calm and trust will help others to remain calm and trust the outcome of a situation to God. We must know what we can do and do all we can. Jesus had the power to raise Lazarus and, in God's timing, he did. God has given us all various gifts and resources to use in ministry. We must learn to be selfless. Even in sorrow and in the face of death, we can, like Jesus, display faith and do all to the glory of God.

God's purpose for this crisis is clearly stated by Jesus, "for the glory of God, that the Son of God may be glorified through it" (vs. 4). Christians must learn to trust the hand of God and know that he will accomplish His glory from *every* situation.

THE CROSSING OF THE RED SEA: EXODUS 14

The Israelites had just left Egypt and were at the edge of the Red Sea when they realized the Egyptian army was charging toward them. They were at a point of crisis. They did not know which way to turn. The sea was ahead of them and the Egyptian army behind them. They could not swim across the sea and they could not outrun Egyptian stallions. The people began to criticize Moses for bringing them out of Egypt (vs. 11-12). Moses urged the people to watch the hand of God (vs. 13). When the Red Sea parted, the people crossed on dry land (vs. 21-22). After God's people crossed, He allowed the Egyptians to begin following them across the sea floor. After the soldiers entered the sea, God allowed the waters to return and destroy them (vs. 27-28). Individuals still face real enemies today that seem inescapable. These enemies may be debt, divorce, disease, or any other of a myriad of serious difficulties. We may even minister through a time when our nation faces the threat of foreign armies and the faith of people is tested.

The response to this crisis was panic on the part of the people (vs. 10). They did cry out to the Lord, but it was not a cry of faith. Moses' response to the situation was faith in God (vs. 13-14). When God acted and Moses led, the people began to respond appropriately and follow (vs. 21-22). Moses called out to God (vs. 15). After he spoke and listened to what God wanted him to do, he obeyed and the sea was parted. This account reminds us to exhibit faith in the face of crisis. Moses encouraged the people to look for God's deliverance even before God told him how that deliverance was to be enacted (vs. 13-14). This account shows that when people feel their lives are threatened or out of their control they may blame their leaders. Spiritual leaders need to be aware that they cannot deliver people from crisis, but God can. In the face of an overwhelming physical threat the best ministry may be to lead people to "stand still and see the salvation of the Lord" (vs. 13).

The stated purpose of this crisis was for God to gain honor over Pharaoh and for the people to believe and fear the Lord and his servant Moses (vs. 17, 31). In the midst of the disaster the people were not concerned about whether or not God was honored. We will most often deal with people in crises that will not look past themselves to see the purposes of God. We must gently lead people to stop and consider the purposes of what they are facing. People need to come to a place where they desire to see God honored even if it means personal hardship. If they are able to distinguish the hand of God in events it will indeed help their faith to grow. In this account it is interesting to consider that God purposed this crisis to teach his enemies a lesson. Believers should remember that their reaction to a disaster may be as much a lesson for unbelieving onlookers as it is for them.

AMNON AND TAMAR: 2 SAMUEL 13

The crisis described in this account is that of abuse within a family. Amnon, the half-brother of Tamar, lusted after his sister. He pretended to be ill and tricked Tamar into coming into his bedroom to prepare him some food (vs. 5-9). After orchestrating a situation in which he was alone with Tamar, Amnon asked her to have sex with him (vs. 11). When she refused he raped her and sent her away (vs. 12-18). She told her brother, Absalom, what happened and he took her into his house in spite of her shame and disgrace (vs. 20). When King David found out what happened he became angry, but did nothing (vs. 21). Absalom hated Amnon and plotted revenge for what he did to his sister (vs. 22). Absalom had Amnon killed and fled from the anger of King David. This story depicts a crisis common in America today.

The response to this crisis was sorrow, anger, and silence (vs. 19, 21-22). Absalom was furious and filled with hate for Amnon and ultimately had him killed. David merely became angry. Tamar hid in shame and never married (vs. 20). Today the response to family violence and abuse is often very similar to that recorded in this story of David's family. Divorce in America has produced hundreds of thousands of households inhabited by siblings related in similar ways as David's children. Many times silence characterizes the response to violence and abuse in such families.

There was no ministry offered in this situation. Absalom did offer support for Tamar by allowing her to live in his home. It is disappointing that David did nothing but become angry. He never attempted to offer Tamar consolation or counsel. He is not recorded as offering any of the love and concern a father and national leader should offer. Not only did David ignore the physical and emotional welfare of his daughter, he ignored the crime and sin of his son, Amnon. Scripture does not record that he ever discussed the situation with Absalom. He probably did not or he would have been aware of Absalom's feelings toward Amnon and would not have let Amnon accompany Absalom to the event at which he was killed.

Absalom was silent, just as David was, but he was secretly and quietly plotting the murder of his brother. If David had taken the responsibility of confronting Amnon and holding him responsible for what he had done, murder would probably have been avoided. When we encounter family situations like this one we are in treacherous territory. We need to be able to minister to the *whole* family carefully and prayerfully. Remember that there are legal issues to deal with in many of these circumstances. Take appropriate action, but maintain your attitude of compassion and ministry.

ELIJAH'S FEAR: 1 KINGS 19:1-18

Elijah called down fire from heaven and defeated the prophets of Baal (18:25-40). After this amazing victory, Jezebel threatened his life. Elijah was plunged into fear and fled (19:1-3). Elijah faced a crisis of faith. He was so afraid that he forgot what God had just done on Mount Carmel. He ran until he was exhausted. Elijah became self-centered and fearful. This self-centered pity is what led to his desire to die. He even requested that God might take his life. The initial ministry in this situation was accomplished by an angel. God used the angel to provide food for Elijah and send him on his journey to Mount Horeb (vs. 5-8). After Elijah reached the mountain, God spoke to him to ask what he was doing there (vs. 9). God revealed that there were many others that had not bowed to idols (vs. 17-18). God ministered directly to Elijah through His Word. Elijah's fear was confronted. God clearly let Elijah know that he was not where he needed to be. We need to remember the power of God's Word. Sometimes we need to let Scripture work to bring conviction, comfort, and healing while we get out of the way. Sometimes, especially in crisis situations, we speak too much out of our own opinions and experience or even secular philosophies. This is not to say that we should not be willing to share our own experiences with people in crisis, but that we should be careful to remember that God's Word is the *final authority*.

This account reminds us that we need to be quiet and listen to God's still small voice.

It seems that the cause of this crisis in Elijah's life was his own sin of faithlessness. Elijah forgot for a moment the power of God and chose instead to fear man. God used this crisis as a time of renewal for Elijah. Elijah was reminded that he was not the only one who served God, nor was he the only one to suffer for God. He was instructed and promptly sent back into battle (vs. 15-18). Believers today can learn from this crisis. Even after great victories, we are susceptible to crises of faith. Christians can learn when the fear of man overtakes them they should immediately go to God for strength and renewal.

JEHOSHAPHAT'S ENEMIES: 2 CHRONICLES 20

During Jehoshaphat's reign in Jerusalem, a vast army of Israel's enemies were approaching. Knowing that his army did not stand a chance against the approaching foes, Jehoshaphat assembled the people and entreated them to join him in calling upon God for deliverance. God responded with a miraculous intervention in which Israel's enemies defeated themselves. This crisis was the direct result of Israel's disobedience to God. Its purpose seems to have been to bring God's people back to a point of trusting Him and not their political allies. When helping people today, we must trust God first in everything we do. Jehoshaphat's prayer was a classic example of the most important aspect of crisis ministry when he said, "We have no power against this great multitude that is coming against us, nor do we know what to do, but our eyes are upon You" (10:12).

SUMMARY

Crisis ministry requires an investment into the lives of others. We must be willing to sacrifice time, money, energy, comfort, and belongings. When people around us panic, we must remain calm and trust the sovereignty of God. We must gently lead those in crisis toward Christ and help them to see God's hand at work in their circumstances. There is never a time when we can simply ignore the situation, look the other way, and "pass by on the other side."

In the midst of crisis, God's voice must be heard over our own. We cannot answer every question and we need not pretend we can. Like Jehoshaphat, we can admit that we do not know what to do and trust the outcome to God.

God exemplified His compassion for hurting people through the life and ministry of Christ. Knowing that God wants to help people in need should send us to His Word for instruction on how to minister to people in crisis. As you strive to help and comfort others, do not forget that the ultimate goal of Christian ministry is to bring glory to God (Matt. 5:16; 1 Peter 4:11; Isa. 42:8).[4]

---

[4]Close examination of passages such as those you have just considered, with careful study of the ministry of Christ, along with biblical commands and biblical principles have been compiled into a model for crisis ministry we call Biblical Crisis Intervention (BCI).

5

Job, Joseph, and Jonah: Three Men in Crisis

JOB

Words and actions reveal our hearts.[5]

Job's crisis was completely unexpected and utterly incomprehensible. This blameless and upright man who feared God and shunned evil lost everything. A total of 11,500 animals died along with the servants who kept them. And as if the loss of these possessions and people was not enough, Job's seven sons and three daughters died when a mighty windstorm destroyed the house they were in. All of these events occurred within the span of a single day. The emotional misery and grief was compounded as Job was stricken with boils from head to toe and his only remaining family member, his wife, urged him to curse God and die.

Worship in the midst of crisis is possible.

In a crisis, a person's response is significant and Job's was striking. In the midst of a grief that brought him to his knees, Job worshipped. This act reveals a heart that was as God described it, upright and God fearing. Job's words confirmed his deeds when he spoke to his wife saying "shall we indeed accept good from God and shall we not accept adversity? In all this Job did not sin with his lips" (Job 2:10).

---

[5]Special recognition is given to Cheryl Bell for the material presented in this chapter.

Words spoken to fill the void of grief empty, but God's words bring His perspective to every situation.

When Job's friends came to comfort him they started out well, simply sitting with him in silence for seven days and nights because "they saw that his grief was very great" (Job 2:13). Unfortunately, their silence ended and instead of giving true comfort and hope, they began to speak their thoughts. When God describes their error He says that they did not speak about Him rightly (Job 42:7).

Grief is a crucible for sinful heart issues.

In the final chapters of the book, God mentions two issues that suffering had uncovered in Job's heart. As he sat and listened to his friends and their counsel, Job's response revealed the sinful attitudes that were in his own heart.

I will say to God, "Do not condemn me;
Let me know why You contend with me.
Is it right for You indeed to oppress,
To reject the labor of Your hands, And to look favorably on the schemes of the wicked?" Job 10:2-3

The biblical record reveals that Job was guilty of contending with and rebuking God (Job 40:2). This was not an issue that God would overlook. In His correction God revealed tremendous truths about Himself and Job responded to this confrontation with brokenness and repentance.

Then Job answered the LORD and said,

"I know that You can do all things,
And that no purpose of Yours can be thwarted.
'Who is this that hides counsel without knowledge?'
Therefore I have declared that which I did not understand,
Things too wonderful for me, which I did not know."
'Hear, now, and I will speak;

I will ask You, and You instruct me.'
"I have heard of You by the hearing of the ear;
But now my eye sees You;
Therefore I retract,
And I repent in dust and ashes." Job 42:1-6

God's power to redeem circumstances is unlimited.
When God brought this trial to its conclusion, He poured out His blessing on Job, doubling his livestock and granting him seven more sons and three more daughters. "After this, Job lived one hundred and forty years and saw his children and grandchildren for four generations. So Job died, old and full of days" (Job 42:16).

If at the end of sorrow and grief, we find a new intimacy with God, how can we not be grateful for the journey that brought us to Him?
As those who read about Job in Scripture, we know something Job never knew. The battle he was fighting was a spiritual one, for Satan was determined to see Job's faith fail. Because God granted permission, the suffering came. This crisis of suffering was truly undeserved, but yielded profound results: "I have heard of You by the hearing of the ear; But now my eye sees You . . ." (Job 42:5).

JOSEPH

When someone sins against us, a sinful response is not justified.
Joseph was his father's favorite and this undeniable fact prompted his brothers' resentment. Scripture records their responses to him in strong terms:
His brothers saw that their father loved him more than all his brothers; and so they hated him and could not speak to him on friendly terms. Genesis 37:4

Envy, jealousy, and hatred will find expression in words and deeds when sins of the heart are revealed.

To make matters worse, Joseph's dreams demeaned his older brothers who bowed down in submission to him, the youngest of them all.

Then Joseph had a dream, and when he told it to his brothers, they hated him even more. He said to them, "Please listen to this dream which I have had; for behold, we were binding sheaves in the field, and lo, my sheaf rose up and also stood erect; and behold, your sheaves gathered around and bowed down to my sheaf." Then his brothers said to him, "Are you actually going to reign over us? Or are you really going to rule over us?" So they hated him even more for his dreams and for his words. Genesis 37:5-8

Suffering is not always the result of personal sin.

Scripture goes on to record the fruit of their envy and jealousy as they conspired to kill him and eventually sell him into slavery (Gen. 37:11, 18).

So it came about, when Joseph reached his brothers, that they stripped Joseph of his tunic, the varicolored tunic that was on him; and they took him and threw him into the pit. Now the pit was empty, without any water in it.

Then they sat down to eat a meal. And as they raised their eyes and looked, behold, a caravan of Ishmaelites was coming from Gilead, with their camels bearing aromatic gum and balm and myrrh, on their way to bring them down to Egypt. Judah said to his brothers, "What profit is it for us to kill our brother and cover up his blood? Come and let us sell him to the Ishmaelites and not lay our hands on him, for he is our brother, our own flesh." And his brothers listened to him. Then some Midianite traders passed by, so they pulled him up and lifted Joseph out of the pit, and sold him to the Ishmaelites for twenty shekels of silver. Thus they brought Joseph into Egypt. Genesis 37:23-28

Through slavery in Egypt, false accusations of sexual assault, and the unjust imprisonment that followed, Joseph's life moved from one crisis to the next. In each situation, the consequences were undeserved and yet in the midst of it all "The LORD was with Joseph" (Gen. 39:2, 3, 21, 23). In each difficulty, Joseph found favor with those in authority over him, and "whatever he did, the Lord made it prosper" (Gen. 39:23).

God's ability to use suffering for His purposes is not limited by the evil intentions of men.

As a young man who was sinned against by every significant person in his life, Joseph retained his faith in the God who was allowing it all to unfold. In his later years, when Joseph was again confronted by the brothers who had so grievously sinned against him, the opportunity for revenge presented itself. The events are recorded in detail as the brothers came before him with their request to buy food for their hungry families. The life circumstance of every person was now completely reversed, for the powerful were impoverished and needy and their younger brother was a ruler in Egypt. And as they bowed before him, he held their survival in his hands.

Then Joseph said to his brothers, "Please come closer to me." And they came closer. And he said, "I am your brother Joseph, whom you sold into Egypt. Now do not be grieved or angry with yourselves, because you sold me here, for God sent me before you to preserve life. For the famine has been in the land these two years, and there are still five years in which there will be neither plowing nor harvesting. God sent me before you to preserve for you a remnant in the earth, and to keep you alive by a great deliverance. Now, therefore, it was not you who sent me here, but God; and He has made me a father to Pharaoh and lord of all his household and ruler over all the land of Egypt. Genesis 45:4-8

It is here that we finally have our questions answered. How could Joseph suffer such life shattering crises and remain faithful? How could he not become bitter and resentful toward all of those who had wronged him? How could he not turn his back on the God who allowed it all to happen?

In this text, we find the key to Joseph's responses over all of these years; Joseph knew that despite his brothers' intentions, God had actually been the one in control. God's plan to preserve and deliver could not be undermined by the wicked hearts of men. What seemed like a crisis of suffering was actually God's provision for the very ones whose hatred had initiated that suffering. It was a picture of the undeserved grace and mercy with which God saves those who sin against Him.

Unquestioning obedience to God in the midst of suffering produces blessings.
As Joseph brought his family to be with him in Egypt, they experienced the blessings of his life spilling into their own as God kept them alive "by a great deliverance" (Gen. 45:8).

So Joseph settled his father and his brothers and gave them a possession in the land of Egypt, in the best of the land, in the land of Rameses, as Pharaoh had ordered. Joseph provided his father and his brothers and all his father's household with food, according to their little ones. Genesis 47:11-12

JONAH

Obedience brings God's blessing and disobedience brings His displeasure.
Now the word of the LORD came to Jonah the son of Amittai, saying, "Arise, go to Nineveh, that great city, and cry out against it; for their wickedness has come up before Me." But Jonah arose to flee to Tarshish from the presence of the

LORD. He went down to Joppa, and found a ship going to Tarshish; so he paid the fare, and went down into it, to go with them to Tarshish from the presence of the LORD.
Jonah 1:1-3

Jonah should have known better! As a prophet of the Lord who knew and feared God (1:9), a direct word from God to arise and go should have determined his course of action. Yet instead of obediently going, Jonah chose to arise and flee. Such determination to evade God's presence could not end well. God's tempest overtook the ship on which Jonah fled as the sea, the ship, and the sailors all yielded to its power. Jonah knew that God had sent the storm, for he said "this great tempest is because of me" (1:12).

God designs suffering as a means of transformation.

Once the sailors threw Jonah into the sea, it quieted. As Jonah sank beneath the waves and into the depths, seaweed wrapped itself around him (2:5). Yet even in this hopeless situation God made a provision. In response to its Creator's direction, a large fish swallowed Jonah, carried him in its belly for three days, and obediently vomited him onto dry land when God directed.

All discipline for the moment seems not to be joyful, but sorrowful; yet to those who have been trained by it, afterwards it yields the peaceful fruit of righteousness.
Hebrews 12:11

Because God is merciful, Jonah was given a second chance. This time when God commanded Jonah to arise and go and preach, he obeyed "according to the word of the LORD" (3:3). As he began his trek through the city of Ninevah, Jonah faithfully preached the words that the Lord had given to him (3:2) and the people of Ninevah believed God and repented (3:5, 10).

Jonah's response uncovers sinful attitudes hidden in his heart.
But it greatly displeased Jonah and he became angry. He prayed to the LORD and said, "Please LORD, was not this what I said while I was still in my own country? Therefore in order to forestall this I fled to Tarshish, for I knew that You are a gracious and compassionate God, slow to anger and abundant in lovingkindness, and one who relents concerning calamity. Therefore now, O LORD, please take my life from me, for death is better to me than life." Jonah 4:1-3

It is obvious that Jonah was well acquainted with God's character and had even anticipated the results of God's truth in the lives of the people of Ninevah. Jonah's emotional response and his cry to the Lord expressed the vengeful and unmerciful state of his own heart. His unwillingness to forgive and rejoice over those who repented stands in stark contrast to the merciful heart of God.

Despite his outward obedience, Jonah showed no signs of true compassion.
Then Jonah went out from the city and sat east of it. There he made a shelter for himself and sat under it in the shade until he could see what would happen in the city. So the LORD God appointed a plant and it grew up over Jonah to be a shade over his head to deliver him from his discomfort. And Jonah was extremely happy about the plant. But God appointed a worm when dawn came the next day and it attacked the plant and it withered. When the sun came up God appointed a scorching east wind, and the sun beat down on Jonah's head so that he became faint and begged with all his soul to die, saying, and "Death is better to me than life." Jonah 4:5-8

God continued to use His creation to instruct and correct Jonah, appointing a plant, a worm, and a scorching east wind to do His bidding. Jonah's resistance stands in stark contrast to their yielding. As this book concludes, it does so with a challenge from God. Scripture does not record Jonah's response and we as readers are left to wonder if Jonah ever truly repented.

Then God said to Jonah, "Do you have good reason to be angry about the plant?" And he said, "I have good reason to be angry, even to death." Then the LORD said, "You had compassion on the plant for which you did not work and which you did not cause to grow, which came up overnight and perished overnight. Should I not have compassion on Nineveh, the great city in which there are more than 120,000 persons who do not know the difference between their right and left hand, as well as many animals?" Jonah 4:9-11

In each of these situations, God used crisis to reveal the hearts of men. One repented, one consistently obeyed, and one, though used by God, showed no evidence of repentance despite outward compliance. Using these truths from Scripture will help us as biblical counselors to understand people in crisis. While the outward circumstances will differ, the human heart is unchanging, and men today will respond even as these men did. Our job as biblical counselors reflects these truths, for we are compelled to speak God's Word and call upon Him to use His truth to transform lives.

Biblical Crisis Intervention

BIBLICAL CRISIS INTERVENTION MODEL

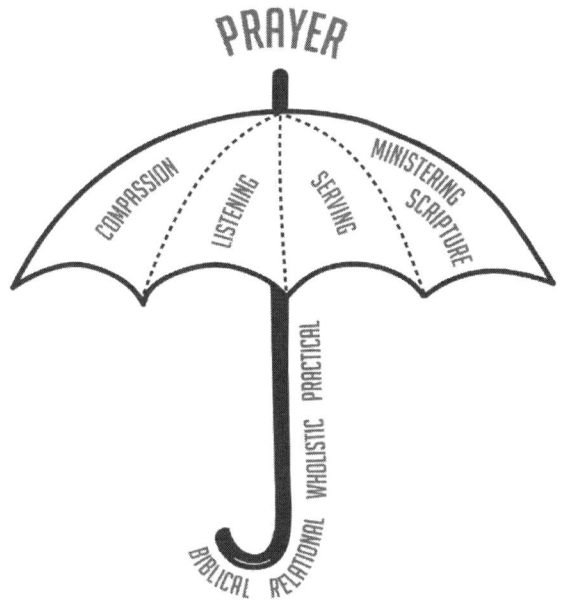

    Out of the tragedy of the Wedgwood Baptist Church shooting, several of us worked together to develop the Biblical Crisis Intervention (BCI) model. The illustration above provides a visual representation of the model. As an umbrella protects for the rainstorms of life, it is our desire to use the BCI model to protect people in the storms of crisis. There are four foundations to the model. These include biblical, relational, wholistic, and practical aspects which make up the handle of the umbrella. Based on these four foundations, the counselor then is able to minister using the four aspects of the canopy. These include compassion, listening, serving, and ministering Scripture. Finally, prayer holds the whole model together.

THE FOUNDATION OF BIBLICAL CRISIS INTERVENTION

Biblical

The model is based upon the conviction that Scripture is sufficient to minister in crisis situations and is superior to any of the world's wisdom on the subject. Biblical ministry does not turn to the world's methods and philosophies, but to God's Word. Below are several passages that deal with this topic. Take time to read and meditate on them carefully. How does the truth of these Scriptures counter-act the wisdom of the world?

He sent His word and healed them, And delivered them from their destructions. Psalm 107:20

My soul cleaves to the dust; Revive me according to Your word. My soul weeps because of grief; Strengthen me according to Your word. Psalm 119:25, 28

You are already clean because of the word which I have spoken to you. John 15:3

All Scripture is inspired by God and is profitable for teaching, for reproof, for correction, for training in righteousness, so that the man of God may be adequate, equipped for every good work. 2 Timothy. 3:16-17

. . . seeing that His divine power has granted to us everything pertaining to life and godliness through the true knowledge of Him who called us by His own glory and excellence.
2 Peter. 1:3

See to it that no one takes you captive through philosophy and empty deception, according to the tradition of men, according to the elementary principles of the world, rather than according to Christ. Colossians 2:8

The law of the LORD is perfect, restoring the soul; The testimony of the LORD is sure, making wise the simple.
Psalm 19:7

     A biblical ministry philosophy challenges ministers to first apply Scripture to their own lives, then to the lives of others. The minister must constantly confront himself to see that he is living the words he speaks and taking the advice he gives others.

. . . first take the log out of your own eye, and then you will see clearly to take the speck out of your brother's eye.
Matthew 7:5

Be diligent to present yourself approved to God as a workman that does not need to be ashamed, accurately handling the word of truth. But avoid worldly and empty chatter, for it will lead to further ungodliness.
2 Timothy 2:15-16

With all my heart I have sought You; Do not let me wander from Your commandments. Your word I have treasured in my heart, That I may not sin against You. Psalm 119:10-11

     Biblical ministry recognizes that the Bible is effective for both discipleship and evangelism. Scripture is therefore effective for ministry to both lost and saved people.

I have given them Your word; and the world has hated them because they are not of the world, even as I am not of the world. I do not ask You to take them out of the world, but to keep them from the evil one. They are not of the world, even as I am not of the world. Sanctify them in the truth. Your word is truth. John 17:14-17

The things which you have heard from me in the presence of many witnesses, entrust these to faithful men who will be able to teach others also. 2 Timothy 2:2

For the word of God is living and active and sharper than any two-edged sword, and piercing as far as the division of soul and spirit, of both joints and marrow, and able to judge the thoughts and intentions of the heart. Hebrews 4:12

Many other signs therefore Jesus also performed in the presence of the disciples which are not written in this book; but these have been written that you may believe that Jesus is the Christ, the Son of God; and that believing you may have life in His name. John 20:30-31

So faith comes from hearing, and hearing by the word of Christ. Romans 10:17

Relational

Crisis ministry must be relational. It is first necessary for the counselor to have a strong relationship with God (Mt. 22:36-38). Ministry to those in crisis is based on an intense, ongoing discipling relationship and not on a professional-client model. It is modeled after Jesus' example and teaching with the disciples. This aspect of ministry requires the commitment of time and genuine love.

And the Word became flesh, and dwelt among us, and we saw His glory, glory as of the only begotten from the Father, full of grace and truth. John 1:14

A new commandment I give to you, that you love one another, even as I have loved you, that you also love one another. By this all men will know that you are My disciples, if you have love for one another. John 13:34-35

Let love be without hypocrisy Abhor what is evil; cling to what is good. Be devoted to one another in brotherly love; give preference to one another in honor. . . Romans 12:9-10

Holistic

Crisis ministry recognizes that it is neither possible nor helpful to try to focus on the psychological or the spiritual alone. We must minister to the whole person. Crisis ministry recognizes God's sovereignty and allows for ministry in both the physical and spiritual realms, providing both temporal and eternal results.

Then the righteous will answer Him, "Lord, when did we see you hungry and feed You, or thirsty and give You something to drink? And when did we see You a stranger and invite You in or naked and clothe You? When did we see You sick or in prison and come to You?" The King will answer and say to them, "Truly I say to you, to the extent that you did it to one of these brothers of Mine, even the least of them, You did it to Me." Matthew 25:37-40

But Peter said, "I do not possess silver and gold, but what I do have I give to you: In the name of Jesus Christ the Nazarene--walk!" Acts 3:6

Jesus answered and said to her, "If you knew the gift of God, and who it is who says to you, 'Give Me a drink,' you would have asked Him, and He would have given you living water." John 4:10

Jesus answered and said to her, "Everyone who drinks of this water will thirst again; but whoever drinks of the water that I will give him shall never thirst; but the water that I will give him will become in him a well of water springing up to eternal life." John 4:13-14

What use is it, my brethren, if someone says he has faith but he has no works? Can that faith save him? If a brother or sister is without clothing and in need of daily food, and one of you says to them, "Go in peace, be warmed and be filled," and yet you do not give them what is necessary for their body, what use is that? Even so faith, if it has no works, is dead, being by itself. James 2:14-17

Practical

Crisis ministry is not just an academic or intellectual approach. It does not take place in the theoretical world of the behavioral sciences or the academy, but in the everyday world of sin, suffering, and Christ's call to obedience. The goal is to minister in practical, God honoring ways.

If a brother or sister is without clothing and in need of daily food and one of you says to them, "Go in peace, be warmed and filled," and yet you do not give them what is necessary for their body, what use is that? James 2:15-16

When He went ashore, He saw a large crowd, and felt compassion for them and healed their sick. When it was evening, the disciples came to Him and said, "This place is desolate and the hour is already late; so send the crowds away, that they may go into the villages and buy food for themselves." But Jesus said to them, "They do not need to go away; you give them something to eat!" Matthew 14:14-16

THE TASKS OF BIBLICAL CRISIS INTERVENTION

Based on these foundational aspects of the model the tasks of crisis intervention are accomplished. They include compassion, listening, serving, ministering Scripture, and prayer. As you read the brief descriptions of each of these components, keep in mind the four foundational principles above.

Compassion

Jesus' life provides the template for true compassion. He left heaven to walk among humans. He saw the people and recognized their need. He was moved with compassion and motivated by love. He took action to help and challenges us to do likewise. It is important for the counselor to prayerfully develop compassion for those in crisis. When responding to a crisis situation consider what it might be like to experience the crisis yourself and what your reactions might be. Based upon this, pray for those you will have opportunity to counsel and that God will help you have the compassion of Christ.

Seeing the people, He felt compassion for them, because they were distressed and dispirited like sheep without a shepherd.. Matthew 9:36

Rejoice with those who rejoice, and weep with those who weep. Romans 12:15

Blessed be the God and Father of our Lord Jesus Christ, the Father of mercies and God of all comfort, who comforts us in all our affliction so that we will be able to comfort those who are in any affliction with the comfort with which we ourselves are comforted by God. 2 Corinthians 1:3-4

So, as those who have been chosen of God, holy and beloved, put on a heart of compassion, kindness, humility, gentleness and patience. Colossians 3:12

Be kind to one another, tender-hearted, forgiving each other, just as God in Christ also has forgiven you. Ephesians 4:32

Listening

Listening is essential in crisis intervention because it

enables us to grasp a better understanding of the reactions and thoughts of those going through the crisis. As we listen to those struggling, we must use open-ended questions to probe their thoughts and heart. This also allows us bring hope to those that are hurting and to determine which Scriptures would be helpful in ministering to them. Listening requires time and a willingness to humbly refrain from interrupting with our own opinions or quick-fix answers.

This you know, my beloved brethren. But let everyone be quick to hear, slow to speak and slow to anger. James 1:19

He who gives an answer before he hears, it is folly and shame to him. Proverbs 18:13

Serving

For most Christians, serving is the most natural part of helping those in crisis. We must look for opportunities to share that our service is in the name of Christ. The Bible gives numerous examples of Jesus serving others out of love. He made it clear that leadership and selfless service are complementary.

You call Me Teacher and Lord and you are right, for so I am. If I then, the Lord and the Teacher, washed your feet, you ought to wash one another's feet. John 13:13-14

And whoever in the name of a disciple gives to one of these little ones even a cup of cold water to drink, truly I say to you, he shall not lose his reward. Matthew 10:42

The King will answer and say to them, "Truly I say to you, to the extent that you did it to one of these brothers of mine, even the least of them, you did it to Me." Matthew 25:40

But the greatest among you shall be your servant. Matthew 23:11

But it is not this way with you, but the one who is the greatest among you must become like the youngest, and the leader like the servant. Luke 22:26

Ministering Scripture

What makes the Biblical Crisis Intervention Model different from the world's wisdom is the use of Scripture to provide the hope needed to persevere through the crisis. Ministering Scripture begins with Jesus' example of confronting people with the truth of God's Word and the reality of their circumstances. Each situation is different and consideration of the situation coupled with the leadership of the Holy Spirit dictates our approach. Sometimes we must minister the direct commands of Scripture. We can minister Scripture by relating stories from the Bible. Still other times, we may share the comfort and hope found in its pages.

Jesus answered and said to him, "Truly, truly I say to you, unless one is born again, he cannot see the Kingdom of God." John 3:3

The woman answered and said to Him, "I have no husband." Jesus said to her, "You have correctly said, 'I have no husband.'" John 4:17

And He said to them, "O foolish men and slow of heart to believe in all that the prophets have spoken! Was it not necessary for the Christ to suffer these things and to enter into His glory?" Then beginning with Moses and with all the prophets, He explained to them the things concerning Himself in the Scriptures. Luke 24:25-27

For whatever was written in earlier times was written for our instruction, so that through perseverance and the encouragement of the Scriptures, we might have hope. Romans 15:4

All Scripture is inspired by God and profitable for teaching, for reproof, for correction, for training in righteousness; that the man of God may be adequate, equipped for every good work. 2 Timothy 3:16-17

For the Word of God is living and active and sharper than any two-edged sword, and piercing as far as the division of soul and spirit, of both joints and marrow, and able to judge the intentions of the heart. Hebrews 4:12

Like newborn babies, long for the pure milk of the word, so that by it you may grow in respect to salvation." 1 Peter 2:2

The grass withers, the flower fades, But the Word of our God stands forever. Isaiah 40:8

Sanctify them in the truth; Your word is truth. John 17:17

Be diligent to present yourself approved to God as a workman who does not need to be ashamed, accurately handling the word of truth. 2 Timothy 2:15

Prayer

Jesus' life vividly portrays the importance of prayer in life and ministry. Prayer is vital before, during, and after ministry. Pray *for* those you minister to. Pray *with* people you minister to. Pray with and for those who minister alongside you. Solicit prayer support from others.

It was at this time that He went off to the mountain to pray, and He spent the whole night in prayer to God. Luke 6:12

Let us therefore draw near with confidence to the throne of grace, that we may receive mercy and may find grace to help in time of need. Hebrews 4:16

Pray without ceasing. 1 Thessalonians 5:17

Therefore, confess your sins to one another, and pray for one another so that you may be healed. The effective prayer of a righteous man can accomplish much. James 5:16

The BCI model provides a template upon which the counselor can base his or her crisis ministry. The tasks of compassion, listening, serving, ministering Scripture and prayer give the Biblical Crisis Intervention Model a perspective that the world does not offer. As the world tries to provide a temporary solution to a crisis, the Word of God offers an opportunity for those in crisis to find the healing that God offers.

7

Responding to Crisis

If the LORD had not been my help, My soul would soon have dwelt in the abode of silence. If I should say, "My foot has slipped," Your loving kindness, O LORD, will hold me up. When my anxious thoughts multiply within me, Your consolations delight my soul. Psalm 94:17-19

Constant dependence and trust in God is the key to ministering through the toughest of situations. Below are several general and specific suggestions for responding to crisis situations and scenes.

CHRONIC, LIFE-THREATENING, AND TERMINAL ILLNESS

People in the midst of these crises face a variety of emotions ranging from denial, fear, anger, depression, and acceptance. Ministering to them requires much wisdom and patience.

Prayer

Pray with them. Organize teams to pray for them. Do not underestimate the power of prayer, but do not make promises on behalf of God. Prayer with the seriously ill should be realistic yet hopeful. It should exhibit faithful trust in the sovereignty of God.

Is anyone among you suffering? Then he must pray. Is anyone cheerful? He is to sing praises. Is anyone among you sick? Then he must call for the elders of the church and they are to pray over him, anointing him with oil in the name of the Lord; and the prayer offered in faith will restore the one who is sick, and the Lord will raise him up, and if he has committed sins, they will be forgiven him. Therefore, confess your sins to one another, and pray for one another so that you may be healed. The effective prayer of a righteous man can accomplish much. James 5:13-16

In the same way the Spirit also helps our weakness; for we do not know how to pray as we should, but the Spirit Himself intercedes for us with groanings too deep for words. Romans 8:26

Those suffering from incurable disease and facing inevitable death need to be reminded that their lives can still bring glory and honor to God as they face death with courage and faith. If it is not God's will to glorify Himself through bringing physical healing, it is His will to be glorified in His servant's suffering or death.

Because of the surpassing greatness of the revelations, for this reason, to keep me from exalting myself, there was given me a thorn in the flesh, a messenger of Satan to torment me-- to keep me from exalting myself! Concerning this I implored the Lord three times that it might leave me. And He has said to me, "My grace is sufficient for you, for power is perfected in weakness "Most gladly, therefore, I will rather boast about my weaknesses, so that the power of Christ may dwell in me. 2 Corinthians 12:7-9

Showing Compassion

This involves entering into the struggles of suffering people. Compassion is often best displayed by quiet presence and a few words of comfort. You cannot answer all the questions and need not try. Point people to God, the greatest source of compassion.

And if one member suffers, all the members suffer with it; if one member is honored, all the members rejoice with it.
1 Corinthians 12:26

Blessed be the God and Father of our Lord Jesus Christ, the Father of mercies and God of all comfort, who comforts us in all our affliction so that we will be able to comfort those who are in any affliction with the comfort with which we ourselves are comforted by God. 2 Corinthians 1:3-4

So, as those who have been chosen of God, holy and beloved, put on a heart of compassion, kindness, humility, gentleness and patience. Colossians 3:12

Listening
  As God's minister in times of suffering, your actions must reflect the character of God. Be willing to listen attentively to people. Maintain eye contact as they talk. Do not be afraid to witness their emotions and share in their pain. If they repeat the same stories or ask the same questions over and over, be patient with them. Do not interrupt them when they speak. Answer the questions you can answer. Respond to their stories when appropriate. Whenever possible, keep the focus on God and His Word.

I waited patiently for the LORD; And He inclined to me and heard my cry. Psalm 40:1

Serving
  There are many ways to serve people suffering from serious illness. Below are just a few suggestions:

- Deliver food to the home
- Care for children

- Clean the house
- Run errands
- Make phone calls
- Provide care
- Provide transportation
- Provide tapes of your church service
- Take care of pets

In circumstances where death is inevitable, you may be called upon to help make arrangements for funerals, to help decide how to distribute the deceased's belongings, or to help contact family members. Do not allow your own discomfort with such tasks to keep you from providing much-needed ministry.

Ministering Scripture

Some of the most applicable passages for ministering to the chronically or terminally ill appear below:

For we know that if the earthly tent which is our house is torn down, we have a building from God, a house not made with hands, eternal in the heavens. 2 Corinthians 5:1

Even though I walk through the valley of the shadow of death, I fear no evil, for You are with me; Your rod and Your staff, they comfort me. Psalm 23:4

And He has said to me, "My grace is sufficient for you, for power is perfected in weakness." Most gladly, therefore, I will rather boast about my weaknesses, so that the power of Christ may dwell in me. 2 Corinthians 12:9

Peace I leave with you; My peace I give to you; not as the world gives do I give to you Do not let your heart be troubled, nor let it be fearful. John 14:27

For I am convinced that neither death, nor life, nor angels, nor principalities, nor things present, nor things to come, nor powers, nor height, nor depth, nor any other created thing, will be able to separate us from the love of God, which is in Christ Jesus our Lord. Romans 8:38-39

O DEATH, WHERE IS YOUR VICTORY? O DEATH, WHERE IS YOUR STING?" The sting of death is sin, and the power of sin is the law; but thanks be to God, who gives us the victory through our Lord Jesus Christ. Therefore, my beloved brethren, be steadfast, immovable, always abounding in the work of the Lord, knowing that your toil is not in vain in the Lord. I Corinthians 15:55-58

There are countless other passages that may be applicable in specific situations. The key is to remember that God's Word is living and active and can accomplish far more than our words and opinions. Do not be afraid to share Scripture with those facing severe trials and death. It is always appropriate to remind people of God's love and sovereignty, even in the face of life's deepest hurts and most bewildering events.

And the peace of God, which surpasses all comprehension, will guard your hearts and your minds in Christ Jesus Philippians 4:7

VICTIMS OF CRIME

People tend to avoid victims of violent crimes, or at least the topic of their crime. Sometimes this is because we do not know what to say. Other times it is because thinking of crime may bring about fear in our own hearts. We may wonder why such victims seem to be stuck. We often overlook them when it comes to ministry. Victims of crime are often in need of *strong* empathetic ministry. They are often struggling with the following emotions and attitudes.

- Feelings of deep sadness, anger, and depression

- Feelings of vulnerability, fear, helplessness, and confusion
- Feelings of suspicion, especially of strangers
- Mood swings from encouragement to discouragement
- Unwillingness to forgive
- A desire for vengeance, which leads to guilt
- Guilt over whether they might have done something differently to have prevented what happened
- Deep desire to feel safe and in control again, which leads to a fixation with establishing routines and creating a safe environment
- Becomes overprotective of loved ones
- Withdrawal
- Sense of hopelessness and helplessness

In addition to emotional upheaval, victims of crime may be facing physical challenges such as:

- Recuperation from injury
- Financial or property loss
- Insomnia and bad dreams
- Digestive and appetite problems
- Crying at unexpected times
- Forgetfulness and trouble concentrating
- Job or school performance may decrease

The challenges of dealing with the legal system often add to the emotional discomfort associated with crime.

- They are often not kept informed
- Deals and plea bargains are made without their input
- Sentences appear unjust
- The whole process may be drawn out for years

Crimes with identifiable victims unhinge two of our most cherished ideas First, the idea that the world is an orderly, predictable, understandable place. Second, that we have a certain level of control over our lives. James 4:13-15 teaches that this is not so:

Come now, you who say, "Today or tomorrow we will go to such and such a city, and spend a year there and engage in business and make a profit." Yet you do not know what your life will be like tomorrow. You are just a vapor that appears for a little while and then vanishes away. Instead, you ought to say, "If the Lord wills, we will live and also do this or that."

Let's apply the Biblical Crisis Intervention Model to this particular issue:

Prayer

Prayer is needed in every area of our lives. Victims of crime may be particularly concerned for themselves and their family's future safety. Be sensitive to this, and make sure that you pray with them for God's protection. They need God's comfort and peace. They may be grappling with doubts and questions concerning why they have been violated by crime. Ask God to increase their faith and help them see past the current dark circumstances. Be careful not to minimize their loss.

Who will stand up for me against evildoers? Who will take his stand for me against those who do wickedness? If the LORD had not been my help, My soul would soon have dwelt in the abode of silence. If I should say, "My foot has slipped," Your loving kindness, O LORD, will hold me up. When my anxious thoughts multiply within me, Your consolations delight my soul. Psalm 94:16-19

But I say to you who hear, love your enemies, do good to those who hate you, bless those who curse you, pray for those who mistreat you. Luke 6:27-28

In the same way the Spirit also helps our weakness; for we do not know how to pray as we should, but the Spirit Himself intercedes for us with groanings too deep for words . . . Romans 8:26

Show Compassion

We show compassion by our presence and empathy. We can assure them that God is with them and that He understands fully what they are going through. They need to know that their feelings of fear, anger, and pain will pass.

God is our refuge and strength, A very present help in trouble. Psalm 46:1

Therefore, since we have a great high priest who has passed through the heavens, Jesus the Son of God, let us hold fast our confession. For we do not have a high priest who cannot sympathize with our weaknesses, but One who has been tempted in all things as we are, yet without sin. Therefore let us draw near with confidence to the throne of grace, so that we may receive mercy and find grace to help in time of need. Hebrews 4:14-16

Whenever a woman is in labor she has pain, because her hour has come; but when she gives birth to the child, she no longer remembers the anguish because of the joy that a child has been born into the world. "Therefore you too have grief now; but I will see you again, and your heart will rejoice, and no one will take your joy away from you. John 16:21-22

For just as the sufferings of Christ are ours in abundance, so also our comfort is abundant through Christ. 2 Corinthians 1:5

Listen

Victims of crime usually desire to tell their story. They often analyze the events, hoping to understand why the crime occurred or what they might have done to avoid the event. They will express their sense of violation and outrage. They may express the desire to seek revenge or may simply talk of the fear that overwhelms them. We must be willing to listen intently. Only after listening to them, can we attempt to help them see the events from a biblical perspective.

He who gives an answer before he hears, It is folly and shame to him. Proverbs 18:13

Serve

We can serve victims of crime in many practical ways. Needs may vary with the situation. Once we identify these needs, we seek to address them. These may include physical and financial needs. Many times, victims of violent crimes incur medical expenses, lose time on the job, or have had property damaged or stolen. Our best example in Scripture is the action the Good Samaritan took (Luke 10:30-35). He provided medical care, shelter, and transportation for a crime victim. For some time after being victimized, a person may simply require the presence of another person to help them overcome feelings of fear and vulnerability. In cases where victims are hospitalized, we may offer to care for their children, run errands, or make sure their household continues to operate. The list of practical ways to serve victims of crime is only limited by our desire to serve.

And whoever wishes to be first among you shall be your slave; just as the Son of Man did not come to be served, but to serve, and to give His life a ransom for many. Matthew 20:27-28

For you were called to freedom, brethren; only do not turn your freedom into an opportunity for the flesh, but through love serve one another. Galatians 5:13

Minister Scripture

Help victims of crime see what Scripture teaches about fear, anger, and forgiveness. Give them specific ways they can put this into practice.

Fear

Not all fear is sinful. Sometimes, fear may be a legitimate response to a given situation. It is sin when we fear what Scripture forbids us to fear. We cannot live our lives in constant fear of other people. Crime victims must see that only the power of love overcomes fear. By loving God as commanded in Scripture, we learn to trust the sovereignty of God over the events in our lives.

There is no fear in love; but perfect love casts out fear, because fear involves punishment, and the one who fears is not perfected in love. 1 John 4:18

Anger

The usual response to being victimized by a criminal is anger. This is anger that is indeed justified. However, Scripture teaches that we are not to hold on to anger, but rather to let it go and trust God for dealing with the offender. The anger of man does not achieve God's purposes. Certainly, the laws of the land make provisions for dealing with criminals, but we must be able to put away anger and allow the system to handle the criminal.

BE ANGRY, AND yet DO NOT SIN; do not let the sun go down on your anger. Ephesians 4:26

For the anger of man does not achieve the righteousness of God. James 1:20

But now you also, put them all aside: anger, wrath, malice, slander, and abusive speech from your mouth. Colossians 3:8

Forgiveness

Forgiveness is a challenge, yet lack of forgiveness leads to bitterness and the desire for revenge. Help victims of crime understand what Scripture teaches about forgiveness and revenge. Forgiveness of others should be done in recognition of how much God has forgiven which is represented so well in Matthew 18:23-35:

"For this reason the kingdom of heaven may be compared to a king who wished to settle accounts with his slaves. When he had begun to settle them, one who owed him ten thousand talents was brought to him. But since he did not have the means to repay, his lord commanded him to be sold, along with his wife and children and all that he had, and repayment to be made. So the slave fell to the ground and prostrated himself before him, saying, 'Have patience with me and I will repay you everything.' And the lord of that slave felt compassion and released him and forgave him the debt. But that slave went out and found one of his fellow slaves who owed him a hundred denarii; and he seized him and began to choke him, saying, 'Pay back what you owe.' So his fellow slave fell to the ground and began to plead with him, saying, 'Have patience with me and I will repay you.' But he was unwilling and went and threw him in prison until he should pay back what was owed. So when his fellow slaves saw what had happened, they were deeply grieved and came and reported to their lord all that had happened. Then summoning him, his lord said to him, 'You wicked slave, I forgave you all that debt because you pleaded with me. Should you not also have had mercy on your fellow slave, in the same way that I had mercy on you?' And his lord, moved with anger, handed him over to the torturers until he should repay all that was owed him. My heavenly Father will also do the same to you, if each of you does not forgive his brother from your heart." Matthew 18:23-35

Be kind to one another, tender-hearted, forgiving each other, just as God in Christ also has forgiven you. Ephesians 4:32

Never take your own revenge, beloved, but leave room for the wrath of God, for it is written, "VENGEANCE IS MINE, I WILL REPAY," says the Lord. Romans 12:19

A Few Pointers

- Do not say things similar to: "I know how you feel."
- Do not give them too much to do
- Do not respond too quickly to expressed emotions
- Do not expect everyone to respond the same way

A recent study revealed that victims of crime expect ministers to:

- Refrain from explaining unless they are asked to
- Not attempt to "take away reality."
- Help them deal with forgiveness
- Be available and "stay close"
- Remember them and be willing to minister for "a long time"
- "Be patient."
- "Remind me this isn't all there is to life."

LOSS OF PROPERTY

Disasters such as fires, hurricanes, earthquakes, floods, tornadoes, and in today's world, even terrorist attacks, often cause people to lose much or even everything they own. Certainly, the loss of all or most of one's earthly belongings can be devastating. Many people gauge their own sense of worth by what they own. Others find their security in their belongings. We must realize that the trauma and loss are very real and painful, but we must attempt to maintain a biblical view of the temporal.

Prayer

When praying with victims of catastrophic loss, ask God to provide for their needs. Do not focus on the loss of material possessions. Focus on the fact that God has brought them through the tragedy alive.

Your kingdom come Your will be done, On earth as it is in heaven. 'Give us this day our daily bread. Matthew 6:10-11

And my God will supply all your needs according to His riches in glory in Christ Jesus. Philippians 4:19

Compassion

Many items of sentimental value are often lost. Pictures, family heirlooms, and the like, carry great emotional value for most people. Allow them to grieve the loss of these things. Not having a home can be a very disorienting situation and may place great strain on family relationships. People may lose their sense of security and feel vulnerable. Your presence and listening ear can help give much needed comfort.

Rejoice with those who rejoice, and weep with those who weep. Romans 12:15

Listening

As in other situations, listening is a crucial part of ministering to those who have lost their property. They may talk about all the memories made in their home as they mourn its loss. They may express fear and worry over how they are going to be able to start over. As you listen, make note of any needs revealed in the conversation.

Serve

Disastrous loss of property creates many opportunities for service. You may be able to help replace some of the basic items needed for normal life. Food and clothing are two necessities you can help provide. Transportation may be an issue if vehicles have been lost or damaged. Victims of disaster will usually need to complete paperwork for insurance, FEMA, or other assistance. You may serve by caring for children or taking care of errands while adults are involved in the task of completing necessary paperwork.

Storm damage creates a great need for cleanup. You may serve by helping remove debris and assist at attempts to salvage belongings in the aftermath of the damage.

Then the King will say to those on His right, 'Come, you who are blessed of My Father, inherit the kingdom prepared for you from the foundation of the world. 'For I was hungry, and you gave Me something to eat; I was thirsty, and you gave Me something to drink; I was a stranger, and you invited Me in; naked, and you clothed Me; I was sick, and you visited Me; I was in prison, and you came to Me. Matthew 25:34-36

Minister Scripture

Disaster victims need to be reassured of God's love and involvement in their circumstances. Many passages concerning this have been shared in this manual. It may also be necessary to help people develop a sound biblical view of possessions if they appear to be dwelling on their loss inordinately. The passages listed below can help show people that possessions are not the gage of one's life.

Then He said to them, " Beware, and be on your guard against every form of greed; for not even when one has an abundance does his life consist of his possessions." Luke 12:15

For what does it profit a man to gain the whole world, and forfeit his soul? Mark 8:36

Jesus said to him, "If you wish to be complete, go and sell your possessions and give to the poor, and you will have treasure in heaven; and come, follow Me." Matthew 19:21

LOSS OF LIFE

Prayer
As soon as you learn of the death, begin to pray and intercede for family and friends who are affected. Pray that you will be an agent of God's love to them in this difficult time. Pray throughout your time with them, and offer to pray aloud with them and for them.

In the same way, the Spirit also helps our weakness, for we do not know how to pray as we should, but the Spirit Himself intercedes for us with groanings to deep for words. Romans 8:26

Compassion
Go as soon as you can. Part of exhibiting compassion, understands the urgency of the need from the perspective of those you minister to. Saying, "I came as soon as I heard" shows that you care and in itself may provide a degree of comfort for grieving people. Like Moses at the Red Sea, remain calm regardless of how agitated or out of control others may be. In so doing, you may help those devastated by death to themselves calm down. Resist any temptation to stay away from the grieving family. Words may not even be necessary, because physical presence alone can be a great source of comfort. Avoid shallow clichés and empty statements. Do not say anything that minimizes a person's loss or adds to their burden. Be truthful about their situation and how they are dealing with it.

Be devoted to one another in brotherly love; give preference to one another in honor. Rejoice with those who rejoice, and weep with those who weep. Romans 12:10, 15

Bear one another's burdens, and thereby fulfill the law of

Christ. So then while we have opportunity, let us do good to all people, and especially to those who are of the household of faith. Galatians 6:2, 10

Serve

The first hours and days after learning that a loved one has died may leave family members in shock. They need people who make themselves available and know how to help in practical ways. Consider the ways you may be able to serve them. Think of how they are dealing with daily issues of childcare, transportation, laundry and food. Make sure they are connected with someone to help make funeral arrangements and deal with any legal issues that need to be addressed.

Sitting down, He called the twelve and said to them, " If anyone wants to be first, he shall be last of all and servant of all." Mark 9:35

*Do nothing out of selfishness or empty deceit, but with humility of mind regard one another as more important than yourselves; do not look our merely for your own personal interests, but also for the interests of others.
Philippians 2:3-4*

Listen

Say little. Allow the grieving person to do most of the talking. Do not interrupt the one speaking, except to seek clarification. Let them know that you are there to listen whenever they need to talk about it. Check up on them in the weeks and months to come, and offer to listen.

Then Job answered, "Listen carefully to my speech, and let this be your way of consolation. Job 21:1-2

Minister Scripture

The Bible is a source of comfort, hope, strength, and inspiration. Its wisdom is ageless. Below are some feelings those involved in crisis may be struggling with and a sampling of verses that apply to such feelings. Remember that the passages below are not to be dispensed like some type of medication, and they are not to be merely quoted without prayerful consideration of each individual circumstance.

For the Word of God is living and active and sharper than any two-edged sword and peircing as far as the division of soul and spirit, of both joints and marrow, and able to judge the thoughts and intentions of the heart. Hebrews 4:12

CALLED UPON TO NOTIFY OTHERS OF A DEATH

Depending upon your ministry role or position in the church, you may be asked to deliver the news of a death to the next of kin. Below are a few important things to remember.
- Make sure you have all the facts needed
- Make sure you know who you will be informing. Get the name and contact information in writing.
- Avoid making the notification by telephone
- Upon making initial contact, find out if anyone else is in the home.
- Ask the person to sit down
- Confirm their relationship with the victim.
- Do not use euphemisms. Relate the information in a straightforward manner.
- Share only the details the next of kin needs or desires to know
- Plan to stay awhile
- Assist with necessary telephone calls
- Allow the next of kin to talk and grieve
- Leave only after they have been placed in the care of a relative, friend, or pastor.

STRUGGLES WHEN DEALING WITH DEATH

When ministering to those grieving the loss of a loved one, there are several emotions you will commonly encounter. Below are short discussion of each followed by some applicable Scripture.

Fear

In the aftermath of death, people may be asking themselves, "How can I go on without this one I loved so much?" This often turns into fear that going on will be unbearable. Sometimes fears are rooted in financial, social, or personal health concerns. Realize these fears are very real to the greif stricken and gently point them toward the hope found in the Bible.

Do not fear for I am with you. Do not anxiously look about, for I am your God. I will strengthen you, surely I will help you, surely I will uphold you with my righteous right hand. Isaiah 41:10

Peace I leave with you; My peace I give to you; not as the world gives do I give to you. Do not let your heart be troubled, nor let it be fearful. John 14:27

Be anxious for nothing, but in everything by prayer and supplication with thanksgiving, let your requests be made known to God. Philippians 4:6-7

Guilt

Many times death will lead to a false feeling of guilt in survivors. They may be considering all the opportunities they had to express love to the deceased, but failed to take advantage of. If there has been a long illness, they may feel relieved. This will also often turn to guilt. If a person feels guilt as a result of sin, lead them to confess and ask God's forgiveness.

If we confess our sins, he is faithful and righteous to forgive us and to cleanse us from all unrighteousness. 1 John 1:9

Questioning God

It is hard to understand personal tragedy. There is usually no answer available to the question of why. When there is, it is usually an unpleasant answer. For instance, if a teenager is killed in a car accident after drinking heavily, it would be unwise to point out the obvious to his parents. Try to lead people to trust God's sovereignty.

The stedfast of mind You will keep in perfect peace, because he trusts You. Isaiah 26:3

For I know that plans that I have for you, declares the Lord, plans for welfare and not calamity to give you a future and a hope. Jeremiah 29:11

And we know that God causes all things to work together for good to those who love God, to those who are called according to His purpose. Romans 8:28

Worry

Worry goes hand in hand with fear. Lead people to rest in God's love.

Do not worry then, saying what shall we eat or what shall we drink or what will we wear for clothing? For the gentiles eagerly seek all these things; for your heavenly Father knows that you need all these things. But seek first His kingdom and His righteousness and all these things will be added to you. Matthew 6:31-33,

Therefore, humble yourselves under the mighty hand of God that He may exalt you at the proper time, casting all your anxieties on Him because He cares for you. 1 Peter 5:6-7

Anger

Anger may be directed toward God or toward an individual a person believes is reponsible for a loved one's death. This is particularly evident in cases of violent death. A person may direct anger toward themselves, thinking that they could have prevented the death. It is also not uncommon for anger to be directed toward the deceased for abandoning their families. Children may often react this way.

Consider it all joy my brethren when you encounter various trials, knowing that the testing of your faith produces endurance. James 1:2

Do not be eager in your heart to be angry, for anger resides in the bosom of fools. Ecclesiastes 7:9

Cease from anger and forsake wrath: do not fret, it leads only to evildoing. Psalm 37:8

Sadness

Sorrow is the most common response to death. Sorrow should dissipate with time. If it does not, attempt to lead a person to the hope found in trusting God and away from dwelling on the past.

Why are you in despair. O my soul? And why have you become disturbed within me? Hope in God, for I shall again praise Him for the help of His presence. Psalm 42:5

I waited patiently for the Lord; and He inclined to me and heard my cry. He brought me up out of the pit of destruction, out of the miry clay, and He set my feet upon a rock making my footsteps firm. He put a new song in my mouth, a song of praise to our God... Psalm 40:1-3a

Evangelism

Be purposeful in evangelism. There is no reason to avoid evangelism at this time. The death of a friend or loved one illustrates for people how fragile and temporary this life is. Non-believers will be wondering what happens after death. This is a great opportunity to share the Good News of a relationship with Jesus with them. Let them ask questions, and encourage them to keep seeking.

Talking with Children about Death

There will come a time when children will lose someone they love because of death. Parents may try to shield the child from the blow, but when death is not properly explained and responded to, the child is prevented from experiencing the loss, expressing grief, sharing in the family mourning, and moving on. Children have the same need as adults to process what has happened and to mourn. Here are some suggestions for talking with children about death.

- Do be honest about the death
- Do help children express their thoughts and feelings
- Do be a good listener
- Do nurture faith but don't blame God
- Don't use euphemisms
- Don't assume children will just "get over it"
- Don't hide your grief from your children

Ministering after Violent Death

Every year deaths caused by murder leave behind scores of people stunned and grieving over their loss. There is usually a great outpouring of love and support for those bereaved from family, friends, church, and community.

However, once the ceremonies are over, the bereaved often find themselves desperately alone with the painful burden of losing a loved one to murder. To reconcile themselves to the loss and move along in the journey to recovery, the bereaved need the continuing support of sensitive comforters. In fact, Scripture urges Christians to reach out to provide comfort in the loss and hope for the future.

Remember that the family and friends of a murder victim may have some specific issues in dealing with their grief. Remind them that God is in control. When ministering to them, be sensitive to the pain that an intentional death causes and be supportive as legal issues keep them in turmoil.

The king was deeply moved and went up to the chamber over the gate and wept. And thus he said as he walked, " O my son Absalom, my son, my son Absalom! Would I had died instead of you, O Absalom, my son, my son!" 2 Samuel 18:33

Encourage one another and build up one another just as you also are doing. 1 Thessalonians 5:11

Rejoice with those who rejoice, and weep with those who weep. Romans 12:15

8

Disaster Relief and the Church

Crises and disasters have many faces. Hurricanes, floods, fires, earthquakes and tornadoes all may have disastrous effects on communities, cities, and entire nations. The Biblical Crisis Intervention Model described in Chapter Six can be applied to any disaster situation. Compassion, listening, service, ministering Scripture, and prayer are all essential elements when ministering in the midst of disaster. As you meet practical needs, remember to be intentional in your efforts to compassionately share the gospel. It can be easy to get caught up in focusing only on physical needs and neglect evangelism.

As lives are threatened and material wealth destroyed, people are often more open to hear about spiritual matters. Evangelizing while providing disaster relief *is* appropriate. People *are* able to make real decisions for Christ in the midst of disaster and crisis. Remember that the earthquake in Acts 16:25-34 drove the Philippian jailer to ask, "What must I do to be saved?" – and that very night he and all his family were baptized. First Corinthians 13:1-3 reminds us that, no matter how sacrificially we serve, if our actions are not motivated by love they profit us nothing. It is essential that all of the church's service be permeated by love, compassion and kindness. It must be obvious to all those helped by the church that they are experiencing the love of Christ through His people.

SUGGESTIONS COMMON FOR ALL DISASTERS

To be effective, disaster ministry must be organized. The church needs a disaster coordinator to be responsible for screening, training, and organizing volunteers for various crisis ministries. When a disaster occurs, the coordinator will be the first one contacted. He should be able to respond quickly to determine the needs and what the church can do to help meet them. The disaster coordinator is responsible for mobilizing other volunteers and gathering church resources, including financial resources, supplies, and vehicles. If church buildings are needed, the disaster coordinator makes the necessary arrangements with church staff. The disaster coordinator also maintains a list of resources held by church members who have committed to make them available to the church in times of disaster. These resources include such items as chainsaws, trucks, trailers, tools, and, in areas prone to flooding, even boats.

The coordinator should be familiar with other resources in the community. In a major disaster, the American Red Cross is, by act of Congress, the lead agency in organizing and supervising disaster response, so in a major disaster the church might have to coordinate its efforts with the Red Cross. Many other organizations also provide assistance and volunteers in disasters, with the Salvation Army being the most well-known example. Many towns have a community food pantry or clothing closet. Also, the coordinator should be familiar with local shelters (for the homeless or for abused women, etc.) and know if they would be able to house people temporarily in times of disaster. A means of quickly notifying the church body of prayer concerns should be in place. This will benefit the church, not only in times of disaster, but any time the local body needs to unite in urgent prayer.

Victims of natural disasters may need many different types of physical assistance that the church can provide.

Those affected may have lost all their clothes and other possessions, and the church's food pantry or clothes closet can be of use. They may need transportation, and a member of the church could offer to provide such a service. Sometimes, the church could offer its facilities or property for volunteers to use as a base for cooking meals or organizing cleanup or rebuilding. Finally, victims of disasters may need a place to stay. If only a few individuals or families are affected, families in the church could offer hospitality or the church could help families find a place to stay in a local hotel. If many people are affected by the natural disaster, the church could use its building as a temporary shelter. Specific suggestions for such a shelter are given below.

PRACTICAL WARNINGS

Christians often fall prey to unscrupulous people when attempting to help in disaster situations. Caution should be taken to guard against fraud, without becoming skeptical and unloving. Make sure anyone receiving monetary or product assistance fills out an application form. Make sure people requesting help actually live in areas affected by the disaster. Verify their address by asking for a driver's license. Although it is rare, it is possible that a person may have lost all his belongings, including identification, in a disaster. Watch to see that the same person is not coming back repeatedly to receive supplies that are being offered to victims. Deal with each situation wisely and under the leadership of the Holy Spirit.

Behold, I send you out as sheep in the midst of wolves; so be shrewd as serpents and innocent as doves. Matthew 10:16

So that you will prove yourselves to be blameless and innocent children of God, above reproach in the midst of a crooked and perverse generation among whom you appear as lights in the world. Philippians 2:15

We must be aware that we live in a "crooked and perverse generation." Remaining above reproach often involves taking precautions to protect ourselves from the lies or imaginations of others. When providing transportation, counseling, childcare, or lodging, make sure there are always at least two adult church members present. Avoid being in a vehicle or other private place with anyone, especially a member of the opposite sex. Special care must be taken when handling donations of cash or goods. Again, at least two people should be involved in such transactions. Disasters often create situations out of your control. Do not let this cause you to relax your standards for protecting yourself and those you serve with.

OPERATING AN EMERGENCY SHELTER AT YOUR CHURCH

For all of the natural disasters described below, it is possible that many people will be left temporarily without shelter. A church can use its building(s) as a temporary shelter. If there is any warning before a disaster (such as in a hurricane situation or in some flood or wildfire situations) it would be best to coordinate any efforts at running a shelter with the American Red Cross and other disaster relief organizations. The Red Cross can often provide some supplies and can help provide meals. Sometimes other organizations (such as Baptist Men) bring in mobile cooking trailers and can provide meals.

From a physical standpoint, the shelter needs to offer victims a place to stay, clean water, bedding, emergency medical supplies, and meals. How a church can provide for these needs will depend on the other organizations involved and the specific situation. The shelter must be kept clean and neatly organized the entire time it is available. The church members must remember to keep a compassionate and gentle attitude as they serve others through the shelter.

Childcare may be an issue for people staying in the shelter. If the church decides to offer help in this area, only qualified adult volunteers should be used. An alternative to providing care is providing a designated play area supplied with appropriate toys and books where parents could easily entertain and supervise their children. Perhaps group game or craft times could be organized for older children so that they have something to do. When caring for children, liability may be an issue. The church should take this into consideration when deciding what services to offer.

If people stay in the shelter several days, they may have extra time and little to do. The church could consider setting up a temporary Bible study or prayer time, and offer an evening worship time. A children's Bible story time would also be a good idea. The church could set up an entertainment area and show Christian movies. The relational aspect of ministry-based evangelism is vital in such settings. Individual church members should be purposeful in building relationships and sharing their faith as they serve in the shelter.

There should be clear rules of conduct posted on the walls and anyone staying in the shelter should know what is expected of them. Do not make listening to gospel presentations or attending worship services mandatory for the privilege of staying in the shelter. Be sure to try and collect contact information from the church's guests so that follow-up will be possible.

SUGGESTIONS FOR SPECIFIC DISASTERS

Hurricane and Tornado Disaster Relief
Tornados are one of the most devastating natural disasters that most communities may ever have to face. The impact of the rain, lightning, wind and the wind-blown

projectiles causes major damage. Results can include loss of homes, damaged and lost personal property, lost crops, lost income, and the loss of life. Hurricanes produce torrential rains, flooding, and high winds, and sometimes tornados. By planning before a tornado or hurricane occurs, a church can be prepared to minister fully in a time of crisis. Tornados differ from hurricanes in that there is little or no advance warning of tornados and in that tornados tend to affect smaller localized pockets of people. Hurricanes and tornados are similar in that they both tend to cause major destruction, power outages, and general chaos.

Being prepared to minister in the wake of a hurricane or tornado requires planning, organization, and training. When the ministry is in place and ready to operate, the church should communicate with local government agencies, other ministries, and other churches to let them know of the church's commitment to providing disaster relief. If church members intend to volunteer with the Red Cross, they may have to attend specific training.

Financial Assistance

Show compassion toward others by providing limited financial assistance for repairs to damaged property, to pay utilities, to pay rent for temporary shelter, or to pay for clothing. Assistance would be subject to the availability of funds and those seeking help should be required to complete an application form. Verification that people are actually from the affected area should be required.

Disaster relief kits can be distributed by the church to the victims The kits should contain items such as canned foods, a can opener and at least three gallons of water per person (water will probably not be needed after a tornado). Protective clothing, rainwear, and bedding or sleeping bags could be included in the kit, along with a battery-powered radio, flashlight, and extra batteries. Special items could be available for infants, the elderly or disabled family members.

Remember to place tracts and include Scripture verses in each of the kits as a word of encouragement to the victims

Work Center/Staging Area

The church can use their facilities for a work center for the Red Cross, Salvation Army and other agencies to bring people in and do the paper work for future aid and benefits. The members can be trained to help in this process as well as providing childcare for those who have come to do the paper work. What greater comfort can a parent have than to know that their child is well taken care of when they are working with people to bring peace back to their lives after a traumatic event? The key here is to make sure that the caregivers are trained and screened so that the church gives only the best care.

Communication

Local officials will tell the victims when it is safe to return home. Information on inspecting homes for damage will be given as well. The church can provide a bulletin board posting messages.

Food

Food may have been damaged by water or just contaminated by air or spoiled by loss of power for the refrigerator and freezer. These needs can be met through use of ongoing ministries like, food pantries or voucher systems. The church can set up a feeding center by opening up their kitchens and manning it with personnel to feed the people that have been displaced. The church can give food to other agencies and emergency service workers that respond to the emergency. If a kitchen is not available or is not well equipped for this purpose, food can be distributed by agencies, such as the Baptist Men or the Red Cross.

Clothing

The local church can be involved in helping to replace, even on a temporary basis, clothing. Through the devastation of a tornados and hurricanes, necessities, like clothes, can be destroyed or lost. A voucher system could be set up. A voucher system would require the church to have a prearranged agreement with local retailers that would honor church vouchers as checks to pay for food, clothes, cleaning supplies, or toiletries. A church could choose to have the items on hand and distribute them from the church property.

Transportation

Hurricanes and tornadoes often leave victims with damaged or destroyed vehicles. A great way of serving the victims is by providing transportation for them.

Clean-up

To help outside the church grounds, the church can set up crews to assist in the destructed area. One way a crew can get into an area, is to assist other personnel such as a chainsaw and tree removal team. This team can be set up to respond with or through the Southern Baptist disaster response structure. Clean up crews can be set up to assist homeowners in cleaning the debris in and around their homes. Special training for how to clean the affected areas properly and safely should be done for the crew that specializes in this area. More information about Southern Baptist disaster relief teams, training materials, and suggestions concerning what should and should not be done can be found at www.namb.net .

Follow-up

It is very important to get the victim's contact information and follow up with them after the crisis has passed. Ministry can still take place well into the aftermath of hurricane or tornado.

Helping Away from Home

Most of what the church is able to do in the community can also be done outside the community. The key is the ability to be mobile and available. The crew that responds to disasters outside the local area should be self-contained. This means that if a response team is going to feed, they may need a mobile kitchen trailer set-up and ready to move. If construction is planned, the team should have a trailer set-up with all of the supplies that will be needed to do the job. The commitment to help away from home will require more time and finances, but distance disaster ministry is viable.

Flood Relief

According to the American Red Cross, almost 90% of damage related to natural disasters is flood related. Since the early 1940's, the U.S. has averaged 110 lost lives annually due to flooding. Most of the tragedy due to flooding is the result of a lack of prior information and education as to what to do in the event of a flood.

Pre-Flood Preparation

There are many pre-flood actions to take as preventative measures that will help in reducing the damage and injuries. The Red Cross and FEMA both have literature that contains check lists of suggestions to implement. Suggestions include filling bathtubs, sinks, and plastic bottles with clean water to save for drinking. Outdoor belongings, such as patio furniture should be brought indoors. It is also advisable to move indoor furniture to higher floors inside the house. Family vehicles should be filled with fuel in case of an evacuation. Attention should be given to local television and radio stations for weather updates and instructions. The church can make sure its members are educated concerning pre-flood preparation and form ministry teams willing to help with such preparation.

Post-Flooding
The church's greatest opportunity for ministry is after flooding occurs. While the water is high, members owning boats may be able to assist in rescuing stranded homeowners and motorists. The church may provide shelter for those left homeless as described earlier. Many of the same relief efforts presented in the previous section on hurricane and tornado relief are needed after a flood.

Cleanup is a major concern when the water recedes. A church can form cleanup teams. Members of these teams should receive special training for after-flood cleanup. Some safety tips provided by the Red Cross and FEMA are to make sure the power is off until a professional has checked out the electrical system, do not use any type of open flame in the house until you have confirmed that there is not a gas leak, throw away all food items that have come in contact with water, boil tap water at least five minutes before drinking it, be careful walking around previously flooded areas due to debris. Helping a family clean up their home can provide many opportunities for evangelism.

Fire Relief
Churches can have a clothing and food closet set up to help people and families in the affected neighborhood. Many times families escape their homes with only the clothes they are wearing. Food can also be provided, either by offering food vouchers to local restaurants, preparing food for the families in need, or inviting them to people's homes to help feed them.

Putting a family up in a local motel is probably the best way to help when they have just lost their home. A church-owned parsonage that is not being used could also be an option that is readily available. If these two things cannot be accomplished, people within the church may have extra room in their homes to house a family, until other arrangements can be made.

In some areas, the Red Cross responds to every residential fire call received by the local fire department. They offer assistance to those who have been victims of house fires by paying for a hotel for one or two days and providing money for food. The local church should be challenged by such actions, and recognize the importance of stepping in to help out more long-term.

Responding to Vehicle Accidents

Responding to vehicle accidents can be a vital ministry. A church interested in an accident response ministry should choose a reasonable geographic area in which they will respond to all injury accidents. Once an area is chosen, a church representative should meet with the appropriate authorities and attempt to gain their cooperation and permission for the ministry. For this ministry to be effective, you will have to rely on the local police department to notify you when there is an accident. Once you receive the local government's blessing, teams of responders (preferably husband and wife couples) need to be recruited and trained. Volunteers should agree to particular time frames and days of the week they will be able to respond. Many of the details of how a church responds to a vehicle accident will depend on the specific accident they are responding to. However, there are some general procedures for this type of ministry to follow.

There should be a contact person ready to receive calls from the police. He is responsible for seeing that two of the trained volunteers respond immediately. He will also begin to pray for the situation. Every crisis is going to be different and the Holy Spirit can guide the volunteers as to how to minister best to those involved. The following are some questions that would help to determine the needs of those involved in the accident:

- Who is involved in the accident? Are there children involved?

- How serious are the injuries?
- Have family members been called?
- Do those involved in the accident need transportation?
- What hospitals are the injured being taken to?

After the responders assesses the needs of those involved in the accident,they will be the liaison between those involved in the accident and the church family by getting the prayer chain started. It is important that they get accurate information to relate to the church family so they can be in prayer for those involved and know how to serve them.

Responders may be needed to make phone calls to family members and friends, letting them know what has happened and how those involved in the accident are doing. They may need to go to the hospital to be there to minister to the families. They may be needed to help with transportation. If there is a death, volunteers may call the pastor. Assistance should be graciously offered, and, if it is rejected, the volunteer should ask if he/she can pray with the the accident victim and respond accordingly.

Depending on the circumstances, there are several things that the church may do to minister to those involved long-term including:

- providing transportation if a family lost their car until they are able to get a new car
- assist family in finding a new car
- provide biblical counseling to those involved in the accident
- provide meals for families that were involved in the accident.

A church can add to this list depending on the long-term needs they see as a result of the accident and the response of those being helped. The most important thing through the whole process is to continually seek God's direction and His strength as you minister to those in crisis.

MINISTRY PARTNERSHIPS

Cooperating with Others
The debate over whether or not churches should cooperate with others to accomplish ministry has long raged. Opinions range from one extreme to the other. Many Independent Baptists condemn the Cooperative Program of the Southern Baptists because it takes away from local church autonomy. The Catholic Church and the United Methodist Church are likely to join forces with anyone that has a social concern and a dollar to spend. Opinions seem to vary just as widely between local congregations within the Southern Baptist denomination. The following pages will present a biblical overview of the concept of cooperating with other churches, denominations, non- Christian religious organizations, secular organizations, and government agencies. We will attempt to lay a foundation for deciding who to work with, and when to work with them.

Biblically Acceptable Partnerships
The criteria for deciding who to cooperate with in providing services and humanitarian aid to people in crisis and disaster is whether or not such a partnership will lead to opportunities for evangelism and, ultimately, to glorify God. Below are some key passages, which relate to the subject of partnering with others and some thoughts concerning their application.

And in the proportion that any of the disciples had means, each of them determined to send a contribution for the relief of the brethren living in Judea. And this they did, sending it in charge of Barnabas and Saul to the elders. Acts 11:29-30

For Macedonia and Achaia have been pleased to make a contribution for the poor among the saints in Jerusalem. Romans 15:26

Now concerning the collection for the saints, as I directed the churches of Galatia, so do you also. 1 Corinthians 16:1

These passages make it abundantly clear that God's people and his churches are to work together to help alleviate suffering and provide for the needs of the saints. Surely this Scripture can also be applied to churches helping provide relief to anyone in need.

John said to Him, "Teacher, we saw someone casting out demons in Your name, and we tried to prevent him because he was not following us." And Jesus said, "Do not hinder him, for there is no one who will perform a miracle in My name and be able soon afterward to speak evil of Me. For he who is not against us is for us." Mark 9:38-40

These verses seem to say that if someone is exhibiting the power of the Holy Spirit in their ministry, they are not to be our opponents, for, if "he who is not against us is for us."

Two are better than one because they have a good return for their labor. For if either one of them falls the one will lift up his companion. But woe to the one who falls when there is not another to lift him up. Ecclesiastes 4:9-10

Partnership can be good when two truly work together.

Do not be bound together with unbelievers; for what partnership have righteousness and lawlessness, or what fellowship has light with darkness? Or what harmony has Christ with Belial, or what has a believer in common with an unbeliever? Or what agreement has the temple of God with idols? 2 Corinthians 6:14-16a

Here, Paul reminds us not to make agreements and partnerships with unbelievers. In the light of Christ's mandate to the church to reach the world, this cannot be interpreted as a command to completely avoid contact with non-Christians. Christians should be careful that they do not enter partnerships that compromise faith and biblical teachings.

See to it that no one takes you captive through philosophy and empty deception, according to the tradition of men, according to the elementary principles of the world, rather than according to Christ. Colossians 2:8

Christians should avoid listening to and being a part of the philosophies of man. They should adhere steadfastly to the truth of Christ. This may prohibit partnering with some organizations and religious groups.

For the grace of God has appeared bringing salvation to all men, instructing us to deny ungodliness and worldly desires and to live sensibly, righteously, and godly in the present age, looking for the blessed hope and the appearing of the glory of our great God and Savior, Christ Jesus, who gave Himself for us to redeem us from every lawless deed and to purify for Himself a people for His own possession, zealous for good deeds. Titus 2:11-14

God calls his people to be "zealous for good works" while remaining pure. Cooperating with some entities may threaten the purity of the Christian mission.

But you are a chosen race, a royal priesthood, a holy nation, a people for God's own possession, so that you may proclaim the excellence of Him who has called you out of darkness into His marvelous light. 1 Peter 2:9

Christians are a "holy nation." Care should be taken in partnerships to assure that we are not prohibited from proclaiming Christ and living holy lives.

I said to the king, "If it please the King, and if your servant has found favor before you, send me to Judah to the city of my father's tombs, that I may rebuild it. Nehemiah 2:5

Nehemiah accepted the assistance of a pagan government to rebuild Jerusalem. It must be pointed out that the ultimate result of his cooperation glorified God.

The above passages are certainly not an exhaustive list of Scripture that might shape our thinking and decisions when considering partnering with others, but they are a good representation of what the Bible teaches in this area. Now we will look at some categories of organizations and some specific organizations a church might have occasion to cooperate with in crisis and disaster ministry, and give some information that might help you in your decision-making process.

OTHER POSSIBLE PARTNERSHIPS

State and Federal Government

State and Federal government is officially neutral in regard to religion. Practically speaking, the government often seeks to stifle Christianity. Due to the large bureaucratic nature of government, unofficial stances toward Christianity run the full range. Take care to know the people you are considering partnering with, not just the agency. Individual officials are often in a position to interpret government regulations in their own way. This could add or detract from the freedom you have to engage in God-honoring ministry.

When ministering in a disaster situation there is often

no avoiding working with government agencies. During disasters of large proportion, the Federal Emergency Management Agency (FEMA) may be called in to coordinate relief.[i]

Local Government

The Bible mandates that Christians submit to government (1 Pet. 2: 13-17). Certainly philosophies, procedures, and requirements vary with each municipality. Know where local government stands in relation to evangelism and ministry. Take care not to lose your right to share Christ in return for an opportunity to work with a government agency.

Non-Christian Religious Groups

In today's climate of pluralism and tolerance, it is extremely important that Christians avoid being identified with non-Christian religious groups. Great care should be taken when considering cooperation with such groups. In a world where so many know so little about genuine, biblical, Christian faith, the risk of confusing people and blurring the lines between Christianity and other religions may be so great as to completely prohibit cooperation with such groups.

As a church develops its ability to respond to crisis and disaster it will be presented with opportunities to work with others. Some partnerships may be beneficial to God's Kingdom. Others may undermine God's kingdom purposes. There are not many easy answers. Carefully weigh each situation. Do not compromise your belief in God's Word. Do not glorify some person, organization, or philosophy. Share the love and salvation message of Jesus Christ in ways and through means that ultimately bring glory to no one but the God of the universe.

I am the Lord, that is my name. I will not give My glory to another. Isaiah 42:8a

American Red Cross

Each year, the American Red Cross responds immediately to more than 67,000 disasters, including house or apartment fires (the majority of disaster responses), hurricanes, floods, earthquakes, tornadoes, hazardous material spills, transportation accidents, explosions, and other natural and man-made disasters. American Red Cross disaster assistance is provided to people in need without charge. Red Cross disaster relief focuses on meeting people's immediate emergency disaster-caused needs. When a disaster threatens or strikes, the Red Cross provides shelter, food, and health and mental health services to address basic human needs. In addition to these services, the core of Red Cross disaster relief is the assistance given to individuals and families affected by disaster to enable them to resume their normal daily activities independently. The Red Cross also feeds emergency workers, handles inquiries from concerned family members outside the disaster area, provides blood and blood products to disaster victims, and helps those affected by disaster to access other available resources.

*The Red Cross is overtly opposed to a volunteer's faith being expressed during relief efforts.

Programs offered by Community Services are wide-ranging, touching the lives of young and old throughout neighborhoods across the country. The variety of services include home delivered meals, food pantries, rides to medical appointments, homeless shelters, transitional housing, caregiver education and support groups, friendly visitors, Lifeline, hospital / nursing home volunteers, fuel assistance, HeadStart, latchkey programs, language banks and many more. The simplest way to find your local Red Cross chapter is to visit the web site at www.redcross.org then input zip code.

Charity Airlift

The mission statement of Charity Airlift is "to provide non-profit, specialist, logistical airlift support at minimum cost to recognized charities and humanitarian organizations in the worldwide delivery of aid to those in need or crisis. Such delivery is not just to the nearest major airport, but to the actual crisis site. They provide effective economical transportation in a crisis situation.

Feed the Children

Feed The Children is a nonprofit, Christian, charitable organization providing physical, spiritual, educational, vocational/technical, psychological, economic and medical assistance and other necessary aid to children, families, and persons in need in the United States and internationally. In 2001, Feed The Children shipped 119 million pounds of food and 21 million pounds of other essentials to children and families in all 50 states and in 45 foreign countries. Feed The Children supplements 1,302,192 meals a day, worldwide as well as helping in disaster relief. They deliver the food to about 4,900 different partner organizations that share it with over 60,000 other groups who work with the hungry. Recipients do not pay for the food.

Contact Feed the Children at www.feedthechildren.org or 1-800-627-4556

Heart to Heart International

Heart to Heart provides aid for people in crisis, both nationally and internationally, when natural or manmade disasters occur. They often serve after the primary phase of relief to areas in great need and remain there, helping cities and countries rebuild, after initial waves of support have gone.

Contact Heat to Heart International at www.hearttoheart.org or 800-764-5220

Lutheran World Relief

Lutheran World Relief responds on the basis of need during emergencies. They work through local partner agencies whenever possible and coordinate their activities with other faith-based relief agencies, through Action by Churches Together (ACT International). ACT is an international alliance of churches and relief agencies assisting thousands of people recovering from emergencies in more than 50 countries worldwide.

Contact Lutheran World Relief at www.lwr.org or 410-230-2700

Médecins Sans Frontières/ Doctors Without Borders

Doctors Without Borders are involved in relief in both in the USA and other nations. Médecins Sans Frontières is a French based organization that delivers emergency aid to victims of armed conflict, epidemics, and natural and man-made disasters, and to others who lack health care due to social or geographical isolation. MSF helps in natural or man-made crisis situations. MSF has tested and stored pre-packaged medical and technical kits in its warehouses and is able to immediately dispatch them to devastated areas. At the disaster site, MSF treats people and distributes clean drinking water and provides medicine and medical supplies. If necessary, experienced water and sanitation engineers and logisticians are sent to provide technical assistance.

Contact MSF at www.newyork.msf.org or 212-679-6800

Salvation Army

The Salvation Army disaster response teams consists of volunteer teams coordinated and directed by commissioned officers and trained personnel who are "on call" to serve at all disasters and civil disorders which place a community at risk or which may disrupt or destroy family security and well-being. The organization provides various services in each region of the United States.

Contact the Salvation Army at www.salvationarmy.org

United Way – Emergency Food and Shelter National Board Program (EFSP)

The Emergency Food and Shelter National Board Program was created in 1983 to supplement the work of local social service organizations within the United States, both private and governmental, to help people in need of emergency assistance. This organization has disbursed over $2 billion in Federal funds during its 20-year history.

Contact EFSP at www.unitedway.org

Made in the USA
San Bernardino, CA
11 April 2015